D0856013

MIDDLE-EARTH PUZZLES

This is a Carlton Book

This edition published in 2016 by
Carlton Books Limited
20 Mortimer Street
London W1T 3JW

ISBN 978-1-78097-752-2

1 3 5 7 9 10 8 6 4 2

Printed in Dubai

Photographs kindly supplied by Corbis, DK Images, Getty Images, iStockphoto, Shutterstock & Thinkstock

MIDDLE-EARTH PUZZLES

A RIDDLE-RICH JOURNEY INSPIRED BY J.R.R TOLKIEN'S FANTASY WORLD

TIM DEDOPULOS

CARLTON BOOKS

CONTENTS

INTRODUCTION 7
PUZZLES 9
The Great Green Book of Buckland 10
Uncertainty 12
Greatness 13
Five Armies 14
Race 15
The Beast 16
Gamwich 17
Mad Bags 18
Aftermath 19
Bywater 20
The Martyr 21
The Stand 22
Family Ties 23
Deployment 24
Bando 25
Mild 26
Companions 27
Age 28
Goldspine 29
Vitality 30
The Singer 31
Intruder 32
Moria 33
Gifts 34
Communique 35
Crooked 36
Will 37
Traitor 38
Ruin 39
The Cirth 1 40
Windows 42
Twins 43
Pursuit 44
Forth 45
The Keep 46
The Rider 47
The Way 48
Market 49
Redrum 50
Spread 51
The Gamble 52
Captivity 53
The Cirth 2 54
The Runner 56
Gorbaz 57

Numenor 58
Fortune 59
The Blind 60
In the Shire 61
Escape 62
Well 63
Menagerie 64
Still 65
Elfstone 66
Things 67
Scouts 68
Victim 69
Innocence 70
Riding Forth 71
Spear-nose 72
Wool 73
Woses 74
Comfort 75
Fun and Games 76
Princess 77
Column 78
Woolly Thinking 79
The Table 80
The Twins 81
Gondor 82
The First 83
Indeed 84
Haradrim 85
The Cirth 3 86
Siren 88
Post 89
Coopers 90
Spite 91
The Nine 92
The Nine Redux 93
Angmar 94
Chopper 95
Dungeons 96
Bunce 97
The Balrog's Curse 98
Confidence 99
The Host 100
Creature 101
Carry Me 102
Burdens 103
SOLUTIONS 105

INTRODUCTION

Out of all the myriad worlds of fantasy fiction, none is as famous or as recognizable as J.R.R. Tolkien's Middle-earth. *The Hobbit* and *The Lord of the Rings* have become worldwide phenomena and fantastical fiction, which had previously been seen as somewhat unfashionable, has exploded today into one of the most popular genres.

The Lord of the Rings, in particular, has had incalculable impact. It reliably tops every reader's poll of the most important books of the 20th Century. Through it, Middle-earth has become as vivid a cultural touchstone as the myths and legends of Ancient Greece, or the mysteries of the Egyptian Pharaohs.

The puzzles in this book attempt to remain as true as possible to the people and lands of Middle-earth. I hope you'll enjoy solving them, and, at the same time, exploring a little of the glory of Tolkien's master-work.

Tim Dedopulos

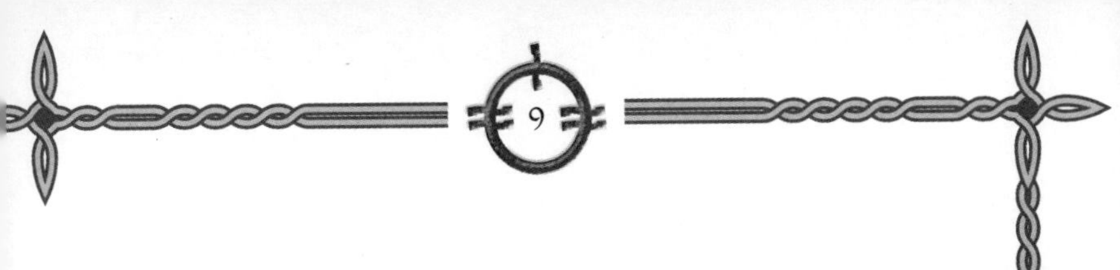

PUZZLES

"The road goes ever on and on
Down from the door where it began.
Now far ahead the road has gone,
And I must follow, if I can."

THE GREAT GREEN BOOK OF BUCKLAND

Fortunately, the *Red Book of Westmarch* and the *Yearbook of Tuckborough* were not the only important documents to survive from the closing of the Third Age. Deep in the warrens of Brandy Hall, the Masters of Buckland kept a characteristically strange tome, bound in dappled green leather reminiscent of the leaves of the Old Forest. Within was recounted not history nor genealogy, but wisdom - of a sort. Riddles, by their thousand, were held within its pages. Some are impenetrable to us now, even with dedicated linguistic efforts, but others remain thoroughly enlightening. A selection of these latter will be presented throughout this work, starting with this early example.

I am a slender tree, although I bear just one sole leaf.
If you let me live I soon shall die.
Kill me quickly though and I shall live a long, long life.
My fruit is but a grape, and yet it fills the whole house.

Who am I?

SOLUTION ON PAGE 106

UNCERTAINTY

FROM THE GREAT GREEN BOOK:

What is that which has been tomorrow, and will be yesterday?

SOLUTION ON PAGE 106

GREATNESS

Within Rivendell, during the eleventh century of the Third Age, a vocal debate arose amongst several of the Noldor. Lord Elrond, wearying of the topic, decided to contact the Istari directly and ask their personal opinions - which of the five was pre-eminent?

Pallando and Aiwendil both forbore comment, the latter on the grounds of disinterest, and the former because he was at that time too busy. But the other three provided an opinion, of sorts.

"It can only be Olorin," Alatar reported.

That worthy disagreed. "Alatar is too generous," he said. "I am not the one."

"It could not be me," Curomo said.

With that, the wizards were gone, back to their tasks. Seeing that discussion was about to resume, Elrond swiftly headed it off. "Modesty got the better of our friends," he told the gathered elves. "Just one of the three spoke truly."

Who, then, was the greatest of the three?

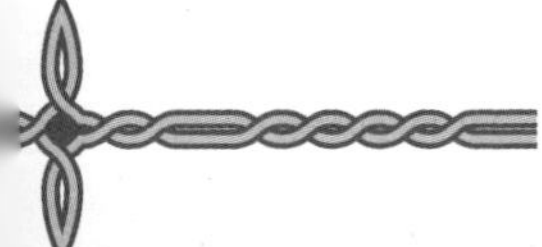

SOLUTION ON PAGE 106

FIVE ARMIES

The battle of the Five Armies, on the slopes of Erebor, was a dark and dreadful affair. Even so, after all was done, and the dead had been mourned, several of Thorin's companions fell to bickering over their performance on the field.

Dori insisted that he had done the best in the battle. "For every two goblins Bofur killed, I slew five. I was counting!"

"That may be," Bofur replied. "However, while you were killing three, Nori over there was slaughtering four. Each one of your kills took five times as many hammer-blows as his, and what's more, three of mine took only as many blows as five of his.

"Forget it," said Dori. "Your goblins were weaker. One of yours might have been as strong as four of Nori's quick kills, but mine were stronger still, three times the strength of yours. For speed, and economy of strikes, and strength of foe, I am the best."

Is he correct?

SOLUTION ON PAGE 107

RACE

Life in the Emyn Muil, the rocky highlands surrounding Nen Hithoel, is frequently short, sharp and brutal. Before Frodo and Sam were found by Gollum there, they spent several days lost within its ravines. On the afternoon of the third day, they were startled by a small, ugly creature that dashed past them, fleeing from an equally ugly, larger-bodied beast.

As they watched the beings vanish around a distant corner, Sam said, "I reckon that small, badger-looking critter had the edge. I don't see as that strange dog-lizard thing is going to catch it."

"Maybe not," said Frodo. "But I'm not so sure, Sam. It was doing a good 12 feet per second, and it wasn't losing pace. I reckon it could keep that up for a solid 5 minutes before getting too tired to press on."

"Perhaps. The little badger animal was like the wind though. It must have been going two thirds as fast again as the thing hunting it, and even if it was slowing down, it wasn't slowing any more than 1 foot every 15 seconds."

Will the smaller animal get away?

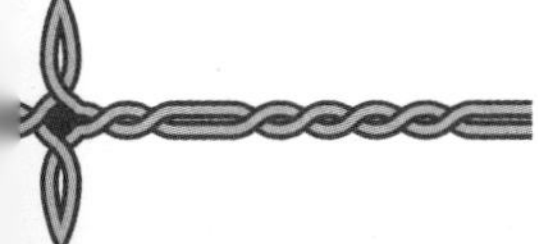

SOLUTION ON PAGE 107

THE BEAST

From the Great Green Book:

There is a beast I know. I love him and I hate him.
His head is an animal, his body is wood and
metal, and his tail is man.
His first is always walking without talking.
His second is always eating without filling.
His third is always talking, if he gets the chance.

What is he?

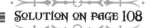

Solution on page 108

GAMWICH

Heading from Hobbiton to Gamwich, one comes across a stretch of road to the west of Rushock Bog. It is dreary country - by the standards of the Shire, at least. It forms an important junction however, offering other routes leading to Needle-hole, Waymeet, Nobottle and Little Delving. So it's not a place to get lost.

In the Great Storm of '63, the junction signpost snapped off at its base, leaving travellers without guidance. If you had come along the road at that time, heading from Hobbiton to Gamwich, how would you have found your way?

SOLUTION ON PAGE 108

MAD BAGS

Late in the Fourth Age, legends told of a hobbit of antiquity who was the richest person ever to grace the Shire. He took his name, Mad Bags, from his treasure sacks. He'd managed to save up 200 farthings, the story went, when he stole a magic pipe from a mighty dwarven wizard. With the help of the pipe, which could let him cross miles in a stride, his wealth grew and grew.

At the end of each year, it was half again as large as it had been twelve months before. After eighteen years, he sent the pipe back to the wizard, with a letter of apology and some fine jewellery, and spent the rest of his life using his wealth to cause havoc, merriment and disruption right across the Shire.

How much money did Mad Bags have when he sent the pipe back?

SOLUTION ON PAGE 109

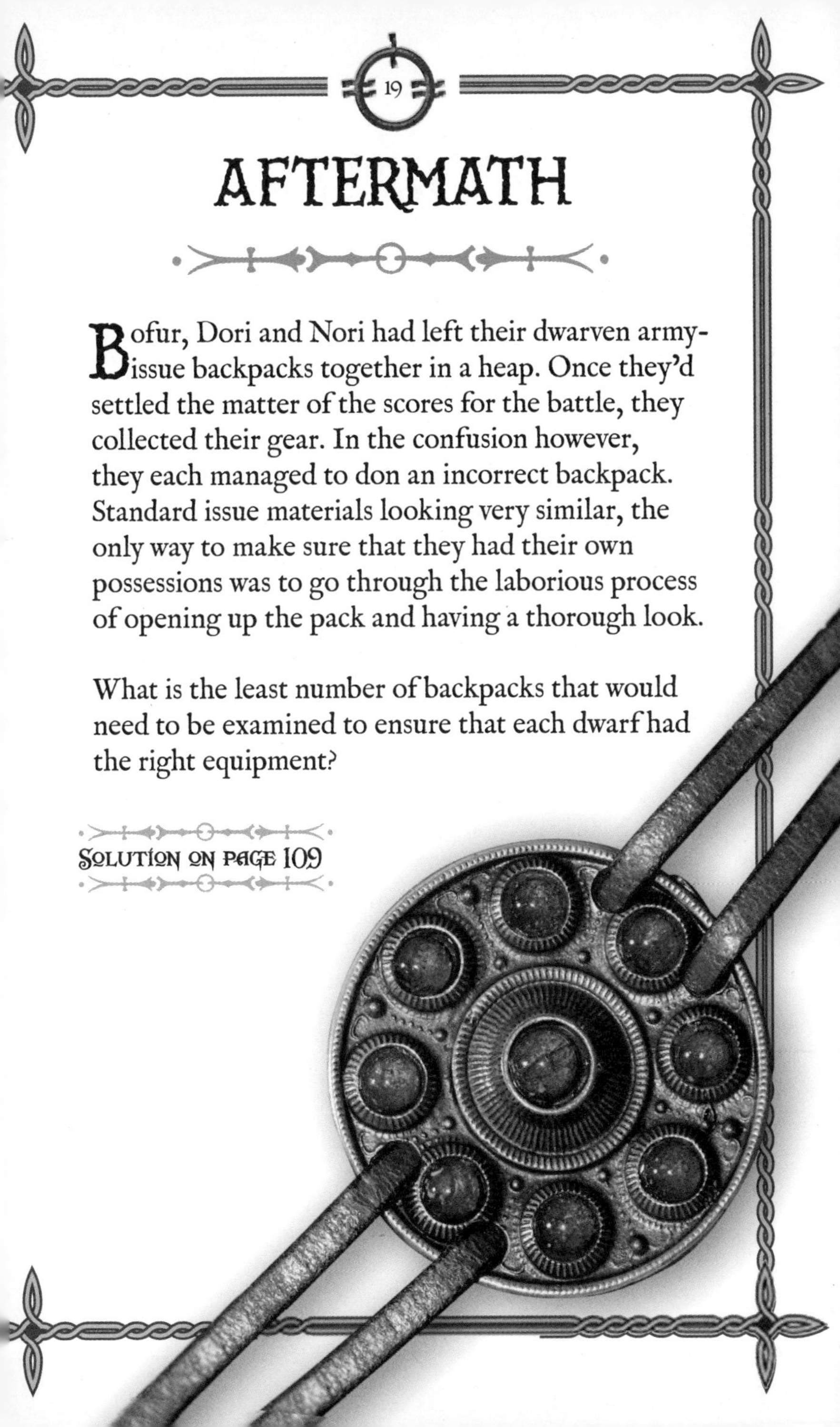

AFTERMATH

Bofur, Dori and Nori had left their dwarven army-issue backpacks together in a heap. Once they'd settled the matter of the scores for the battle, they collected their gear. In the confusion however, they each managed to don an incorrect backpack. Standard issue materials looking very similar, the only way to make sure that they had their own possessions was to go through the laborious process of opening up the pack and having a thorough look.

What is the least number of backpacks that would need to be examined to ensure that each dwarf had the right equipment?

SOLUTION ON PAGE 109

BYWATER

Gandalf had great fondness for hobbits, and took enjoyment from their foibles as much as from their charms. One quiet afternoon, before all that nastiness with the rings started, he was sitting outside the Ivy Bush Inn at Bywater, smoking a pipe and listening to the ramblings of an elderly gent most disgruntled with his clan. It didn't help matters that the old hobbit, Colm Crooktoe, was suffering lapses of memory, and the targets of his ire had become somewhat confused.

"Honestly, they're all useless," the old hobbit said. "Hob's so simple, I wouldn't trust him to open a keg of ale without supervision. Did I say Hob? That's Bom. No, wait... Oh, well, one or t'other. Then there's Tod, whose head is about five sizes too big for anyone's comfort. A right know-it-all. Or is that Ron? Or Hob? Bah. Bom's got a terrible temper on him, unless that's Hob. Or Tod. Lucky he's as weak as old grass. And that Ron's a useless drunkard, that's for sure. Well, him or Bom. Like I said, useless. Lucky they've got me to keep 'em straight."

Lucky indeed. Which hobbit was guilty of which sin in Old Colm's eyes?

SOLUTION ON PAGE 110

THE MARTYR

From the Great Green Book:

It gapes all day and all night long,
awaiting its punishment.
When the hammer-blows fall, again and
again, it never flinches.
It is prized by maids and mothers alike,
who make fierce use of it.
Sometimes moist, sometimes dry,
sometimes empty, sometimes full.

What is it?

Solution on page 110

THE STAND

From the Great Green Book:

If I stand, what will be the first that steps?

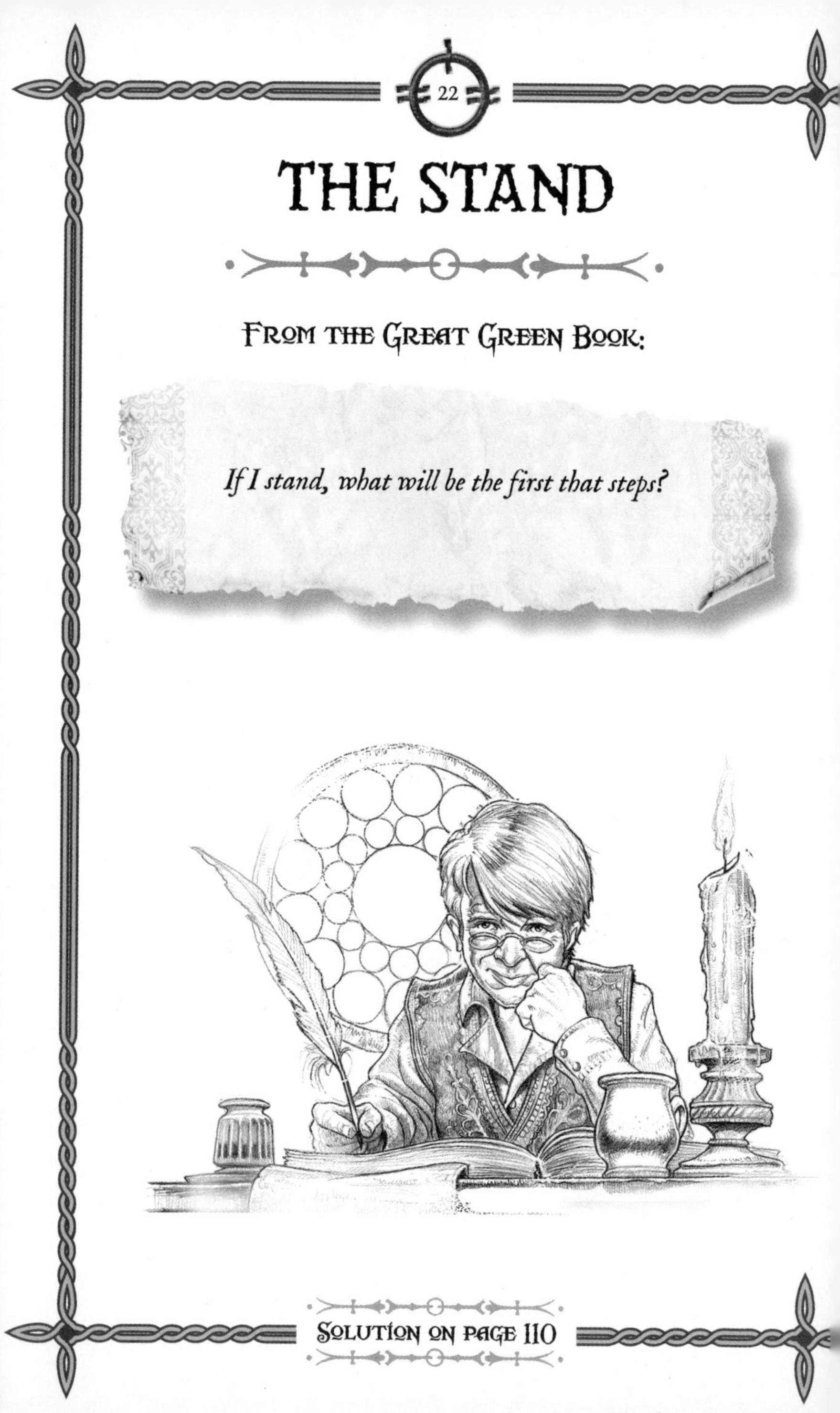

Solution on page 110

FAMILY TIES

Hobbits are well known for their love of ancestry and family detail. Strong roots are important in the weathering of storms, and that is as true of communities as it is of oak trees. So it will come as no surprise to learn that one long summer evening, Hamfast Gamgee and his son Samwise were sitting in the Green Dragon and pondering the intricacies of their distant relations.

“The thing is, Gaffer,” Sam said. “I know that Nick Cotton’s daughter Rowan is my third cousin once removed. That’s fine. What I’m having trouble with is working out what relation her grandmother is going to be to my daughter.”

“Grandmother, obviously,” Hamfast said. “On account of Nick being your Rosie’s brother.”

Sam shook his head stubbornly. “No! On my side, I mean. On Rosie’s side, Rowan’s my niece after all.”

What is the relationship?

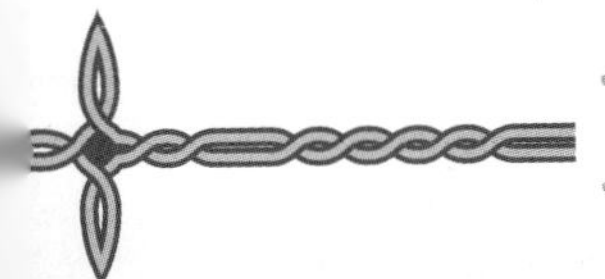
SOLUTION ON PAGE 111
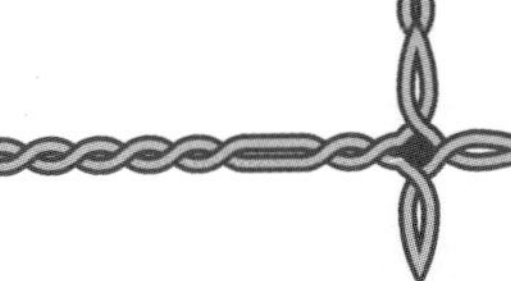

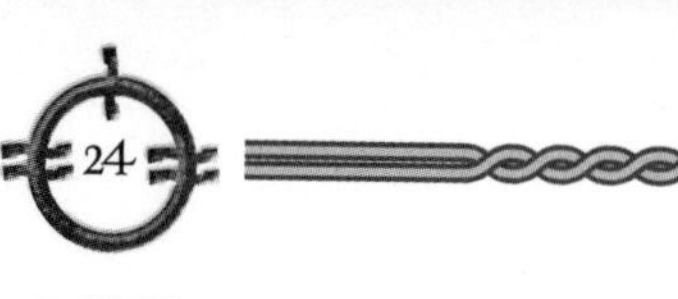

DEPLOYMENT

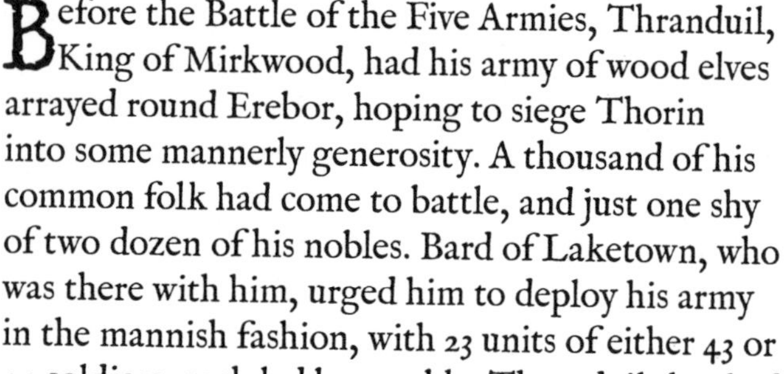

Before the Battle of the Five Armies, Thranduil, King of Mirkwood, had his army of wood elves arrayed round Erebor, hoping to siege Thorin into some mannerly generosity. A thousand of his common folk had come to battle, and just one shy of two dozen of his nobles. Bard of Laketown, who was there with him, urged him to deploy his army in the mannish fashion, with 23 units of either 43 or 44 soldiers, each led by a noble. Thranduil thanked Bard for his suggestion, but preferred a system of his own devising. "In this way," the elf king said, "I have but ten units, and I can muster any number of fighters in one place at need, from one to all, without having to split any of my units."

How were the elvish forces deployed?

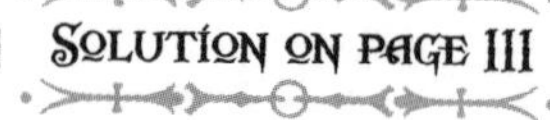

SOLUTION ON PAGE 111

BANDO

Young Bando was dismayed, and his friend Erling wasn't being much help.

"I had three apples," Bando said. "Add the peach to them, and they weighed the same as ten plums."

"Right," said Erling.

"So take the peach on its own, and it weighed the same as six plums and one of the apples."

"If'n you say so."

Bando sighed. "So how many plums alone would the peach weigh? That's what I want to know."

Erling belched quietly. "No idea. Tasty, though."

What's the answer?

SOLUTION ON PAGE 112

MILD

"Oh dear, oh dear," said Bilbo, running around in a tizzy. Bag End was full of dwarves, and they seemed determined to eat and drink him out of house and home. Particularly drink.

He dashed to the kitchen, and prepared a quart pitcher of dark and a pitcher of mild. Distracted by a sudden demand for butter and the sound of furniture breaking, he absent-mindedly picked up the mild and poured some into the dark. Cursing all dwarves and wizards, he put the mild back down, and, using the adulterated pitcher of dark, filled it until both pitchers were back to holding a quart exactly.

As he carried the pitchers back out to the dwarves, he found himself wondering whether there was now more mild in the dark, or more dark in the mild.

Which was it?

SOLUTION ON PAGE 112

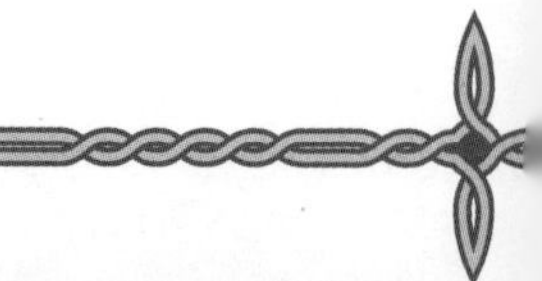

COMPANIONS

FROM THE GREAT GREEN BOOK:

There are four great friends.
Inseparable, they are.
Rarely do they see each other.
They have existed since the beginning of the world.

Who are they?

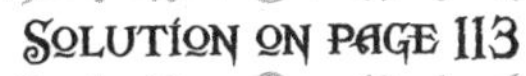

SOLUTION ON PAGE 113

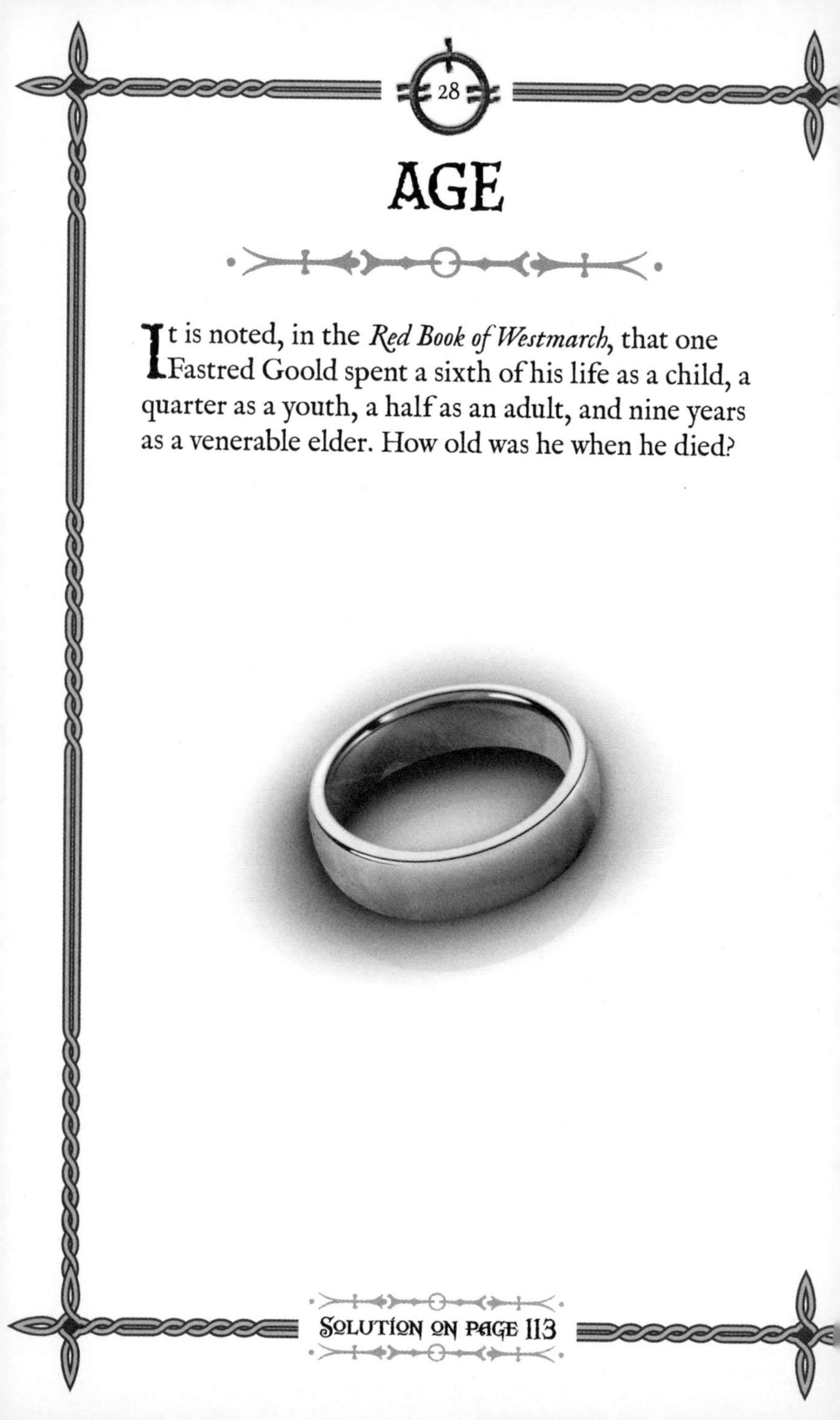

AGE

It is noted, in the *Red Book of Westmarch*, that one Fastred Goold spent a sixth of his life as a child, a quarter as a youth, a half as an adult, and nine years as a venerable elder. How old was he when he died?

Solution on page 113

GOLDSPINE

"'Ere, they do say that Troga Goldspine -"

"Who?"

"Troga Goldspine. They say he's so wise and wicked that he knows the tongue of men, and although he can't speak, he'll give gestures for yes and no. Even so, he tells the truth to some, and lies to others, and sticks to one or t'other for each person he meets."

"That's wise and wicked, is it?"

"I s'pose. It's certainly confusing."

"Nah, it's easy. I could work out what he was trying to say with one question."

Could you?

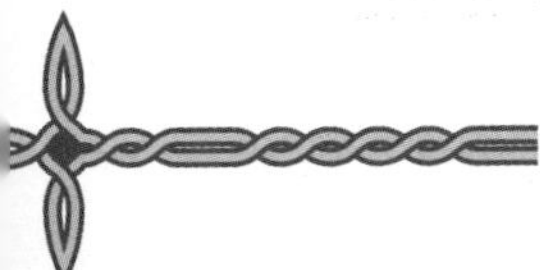

SOLUTION ON PAGE 113

VITALITY

From the Great Green Book:

The larger it grows, the lighter it becomes.

What is it?

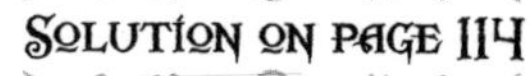

Solution on page 114

THE SINGER

From the Great Green Book:

My body slight, my head in white,
With cord I'm laced around.
Often hit hard, right through the yard,
Cross fields and on the mound.
My voice is heard across the world,
Where urgency must lie.
I bid them come, to dance and hum,
To march and stand and die.

What am I?

Solution on page 114

INTRUDER

Poloc Pott was sitting on the village green in Scary whiling away the day when his friend Saradas ran up to him, all breathless.

"Poloc, you've got to get yourself home right this instant. Your missus, Prisca, is right this minute in bed with a stranger!"

Poloc went pale, and charged home as swiftly as he could. Rushing upstairs, he found that Saradas was absolutely right. Prisca was there, barely clothed, embracing someone he'd never seen before. He grinned hugely, and leapt onto the bed to join them.

How come?

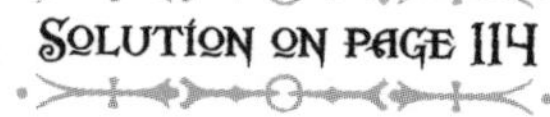
SOLUTION ON PAGE 114

MORIA

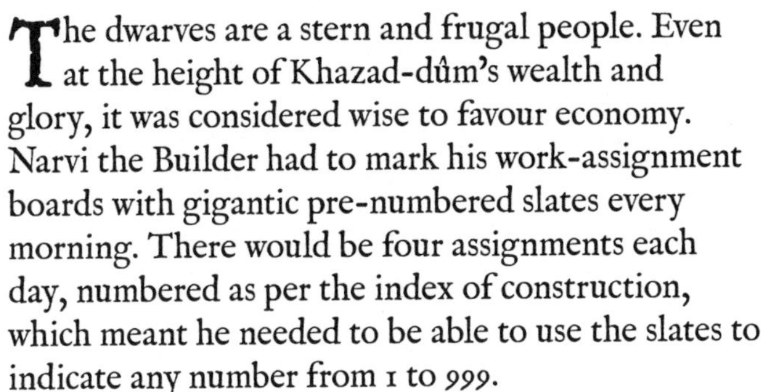

The dwarves are a stern and frugal people. Even at the height of Khazad-dûm's wealth and glory, it was considered wise to favour economy. Narvi the Builder had to mark his work-assignment boards with gigantic pre-numbered slates every morning. There would be four assignments each day, numbered as per the index of construction, which meant he needed to be able to use the slates to indicate any number from 1 to 999.

What is the least number of slates that can be used?

Solution on page 115

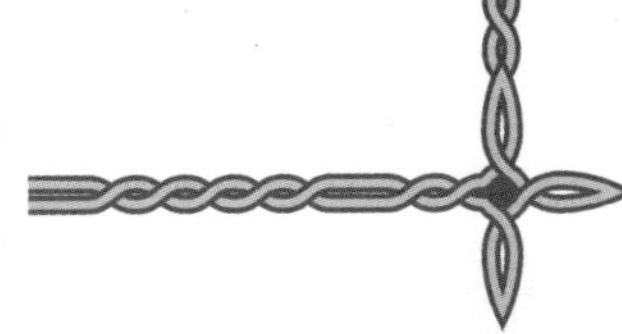

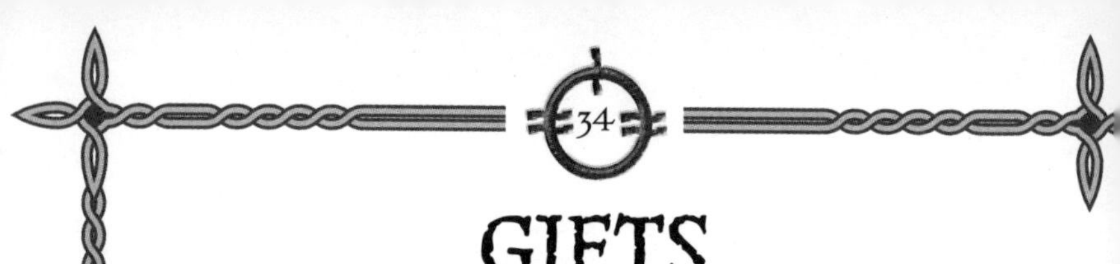

GIFTS

From the Great Green Book:

The one who orders it does not want it.
The one who has it, it is not his to give.
The one who owns it does not care about it.

What is it?

Solution on page 115

COMMUNIQUE

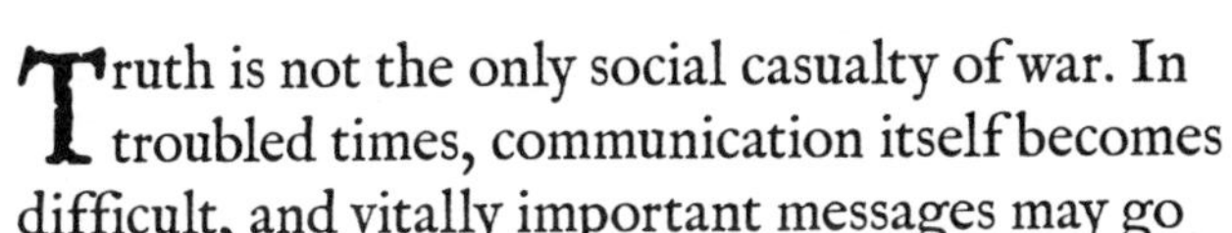

Truth is not the only social casualty of war. In troubled times, communication itself becomes difficult, and vitally important messages may go astray.

Even before the great war at the end of the Third Age, letters were an often-unpredictable thing. As the situation deteriorated, it was estimated that one letter in every six failed to reach its destination, sometimes with highly unfortunate consequences.

So what was the true chance of receiving a reply to a letter sent?

SOLUTION ON PAGE 116

CROOKED

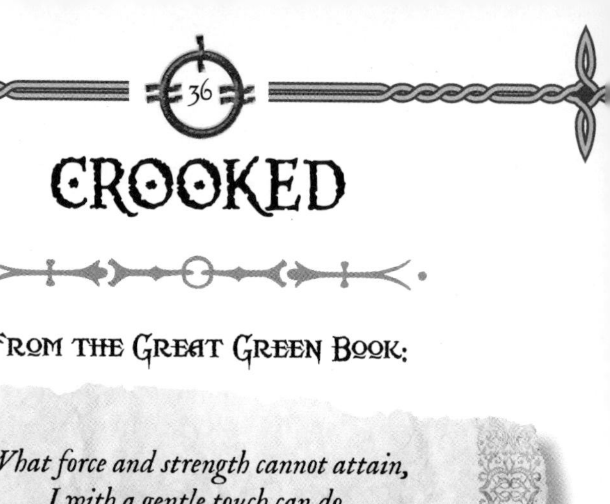

From the Great Green Book:

What force and strength cannot attain,
I with a gentle touch can do.
There's many who would stand and stare,
Were I, their friend, not at hand too.

Who am I?

Solution on page 116

WILL

Araphor of Arthedain held back the witch-king's armies in his youth, and ruled Arnor for the best part of two centuries, but as he aged, he grew somewhat whimsical. When the time came to prepare his will, he determined to provide one last vexatious jest.

He assembled a grand chest of fifteen hundred gold pieces - truly, a kingly sum - and left it with some rather tricky instructions. Each specific bequest was tied to one particular number, which he refused to identify. This number was to serve as the square root of his eldest son's bequest, one half of his daughter's bequest, two gold less than his chief advisor's bequest, exactly his younger son's bequest, two gold more than his wife's bequest, two times his steward's bequest, and the square of the sum set aside for his modest funeral requirements.

How much did each receive?

SOLUTION ON PAGE 116

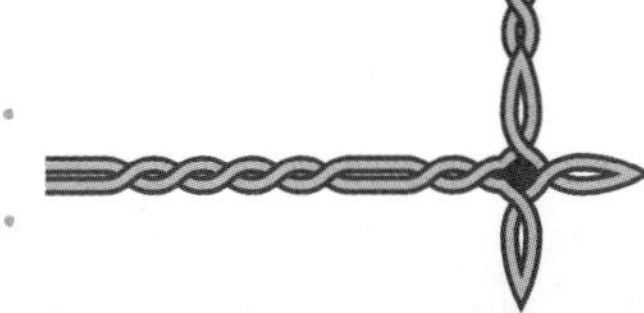

TRAITOR

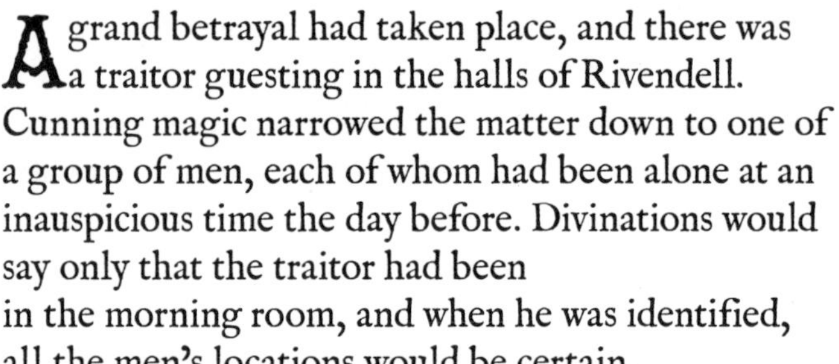

A grand betrayal had taken place, and there was a traitor guesting in the halls of Rivendell. Cunning magic narrowed the matter down to one of a group of men, each of whom had been alone at an inauspicious time the day before. Divinations would say only that the traitor had been in the morning room, and when he was identified, all the men's locations would be certain.

It was known that Valacar was either in the upper gardens, the great hall, or the grand balcony. Likewise, the others were also uncertain. Castagir was in the morning room, or the upper gardens. Ostoher was in the great hall, upper gardens, or feast hall. Anardil was in the feast hall, the morning room, or the upper gardens. Sirion was in the great hall, library, grand balcony, or morning room. Tarond, finally, was in the upper gardens, library, feast hall or grand balcony.

Which man is the traitor?

SOLUTIONS ON PAGE 117

RUIN

From the Great Green Book:

There was a lady with a sweet,
crisp kiss who said to a gentleman
"If you love me, it will harm you."

Who is she?

THE CIRTH I

Dwarfish rune-boards were commonly encoded with junk information to make translation difficult. Before proper decoding could begin, it was necessary to remove the extra runes. This was accomplished by ensuring that each column and row had no more than one instance of any given runic symbol. Extra runes had to be deleted from each column and row, with the extra rules that no two deleted runes could be horizontally or vertically adjacent, and that the main, undeleted runes had to form one single sprawling group of horizontally and/or vertically touching runes.

Can you remove the junk information from this board?

SOLUTION ON PAGE 118

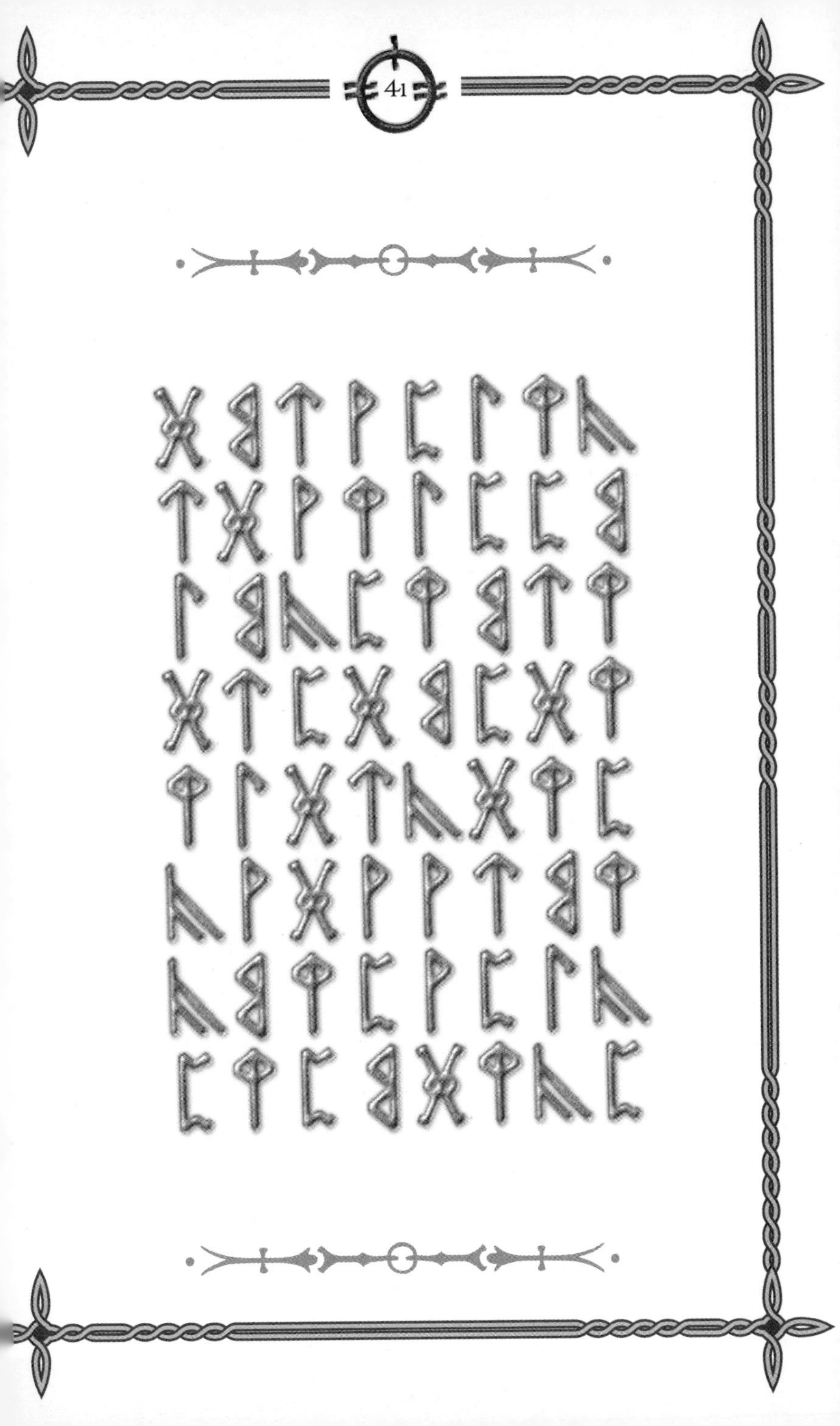

WINDOWS

From the Great Green Book:

There are seven windows, but only three shut.
Good things and bad go in and out.
Two clap and clap, but the neighbours never hear.

What are they?

Solution on page 119

TWINS

Nori and Noli were twins, as identical as could be, and like many such they took great pleasure in dressing and styling themselves to be exactly the same. The only real difference between them was that Nori always told the truth, and Noli always lied. Dotur had heard of the pair, so when he encountered them at last, one morning, he was swift to introduce himself. Then, inevitably, he turned to the twin on the left and said "So which are you, then? The honest one?" The twin on the right smiled wryly, and said "He'll tell you 'yes', that one."

Which was Nori?

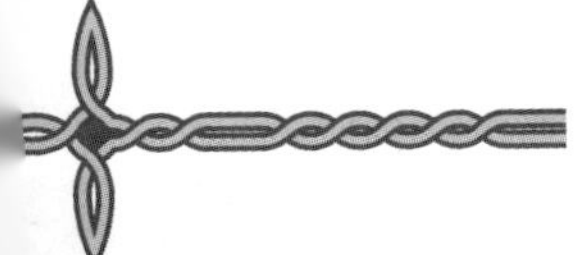

SOLUTION ON PAGE 119

PURSUIT

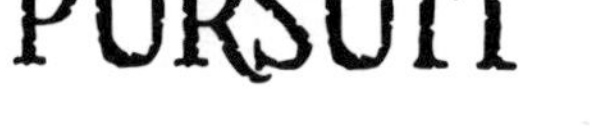

FROM THE GREAT GREEN BOOK:

Ever running on my race,
Never staying at one place.
Through the world I make my tour,
Everywhere at the same hour.
If you please to spell my name,
Reversed or forward it's the same.

What is it?

SOLUTION ON PAGE 120

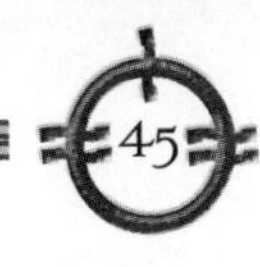

FORTH

Three prisoners were huddled in an unhappy pack in the guardhouse at Edoras. The soldier interviewing them had managed to ascertain that one was compulsively honest, and another a habitual liar, while the third was as unpredictable as any normal man. The soldier had not yet managed to ascertain their respective honesties.

"I'm not the truthful one," said the first.
"I'm not the liar," said the second.
"I'm not the unpredictable one," said the third.

Which is which?

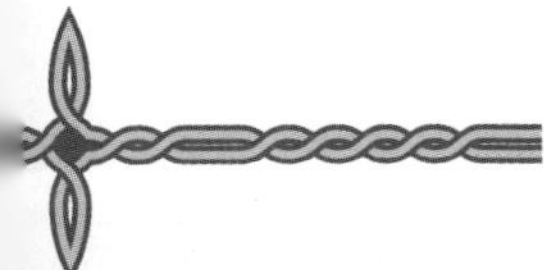

Solution on page 120

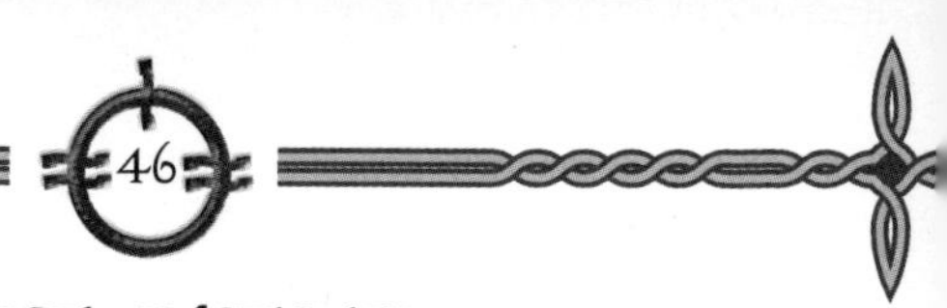

THE KEEP

From the Great Green Book:

There is a palace full of rooms,
each room contains a priest.
Each of the rooms is as the last,
invited to the feast.

What am I?

Solution on page 120

THE RIDER

"The young idiot nearly rode me down!" The old man stood at the corner, quavering with indignation. "Reckless he is, that one. Shocking behaviour. There's no need for that sort of speed on a quiet lane like this. He was round this corner after I'd gone no more than 52 paces. It took me 312 more steps to get here, and of course he's long gone. No respect, these youngsters. I'm not dawdling, either. I'm walking a nice, sensible 3 miles an hour. It wasn't like that in my day, I tell you now."

How fast is the rider going?

SOLUTION ON PAGE 121

THE WAY

From the Great Green Book:

Those who take me improve, be their
task what it may,
Those who have me are sorrowful through
the long day;
I am hated alike by the foolish and wise,
Yet without me none ever to eminence rise.

Who am I?

Solution on page 121

MARKET

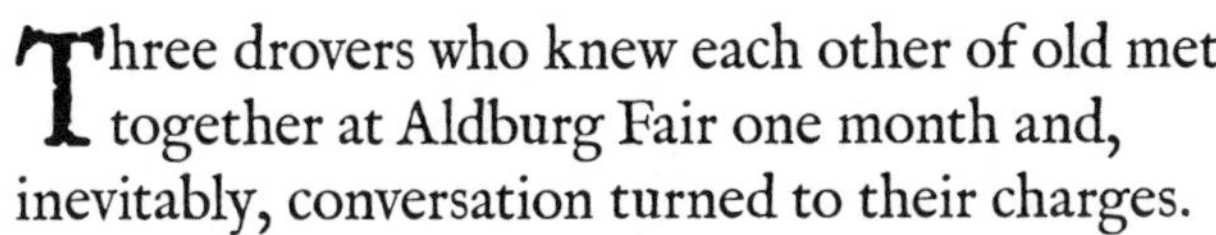

Three drovers who knew each other of old met together at Aldburg Fair one month and, inevitably, conversation turned to their charges.

"If I swapped six pigs for the horse you rode in on, Ceorl, you'd have twice as many animals as I did," Fram said.

Ceorl nodded. "And Baldor, if I swapped you four cows for your horse, you'd have six times my headcount."

"As may be, but if I swapped fourteen sheep for Fram's horse, he'd have three times the animals I did," said Baldor.

Then they shared a good laugh at the idea of swapping a horse for some farm animals. But how many animals did each man have?

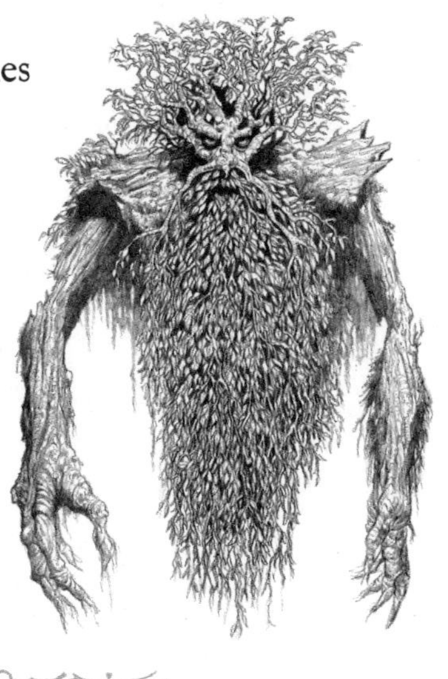

SOLUTION ON PAGE 122

REDRUM

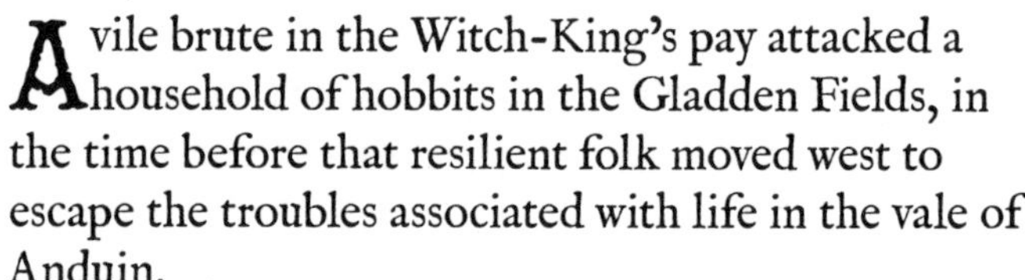

A vile brute in the Witch-King's pay attacked a household of hobbits in the Gladden Fields, in the time before that resilient folk moved west to escape the troubles associated with life in the vale of Anduin.

In the manner of hobbits, a thorough accounting of the lost was made, and the news passed around that two grandparents, four parents, four children, two parents-in-law, one brother, two sisters, two sons, two daughters, one daughter-in-law and three grandchildren had all been killed.

A fell deed, for sure - but what is the least number of victims the murderer could have claimed?

Solution on page 122

SPREAD

From the Great Green Book:

The pond dried up, and the frog died.
As he died, night fell.

Who am I?

Solution on page 123

THE GAMBLE

Following a peculiarly powerful dream, Uthred woke certain that one of four riders was going to win the Mark-race that afternoon. Following the dream's guidance, he placed separate wagers on each of the four, at 4-1, 5-1, 6-1, and 7-1. Whichever won, he would be sure to make a profit of 101 shillings, even though his winning stake would not be returned.

How much did he wager on the four?

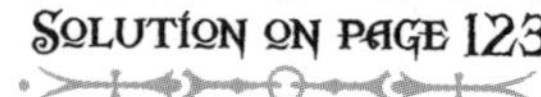

SOLUTION ON PAGE 123

CAPTIVITY

From the Great Green Book:

We travel much, yet prisoners are,
And sternly sharp, to boot;
We with the swiftest horse keep pace,
Yet always go a-foot.

What are we?

Solution on page 123

THE CIRTH 2

Dwarfish rune-boards were commonly encoded with junk information to make translation difficult. Before proper decoding could begin, it was necessary to remove the extra runes. This was accomplished by ensuring that each column and row had no more than one instance of any given runic symbol. Extra runes had to be deleted from each column and row, with the extra rules that no two deleted runes could be horizontally or vertically adjacent, and that the main, undeleted runes had to form one single sprawling group of horizontally and/or vertically touching runes.

Can you remove the junk information from this board?

SOLUTION ON PAGE 124

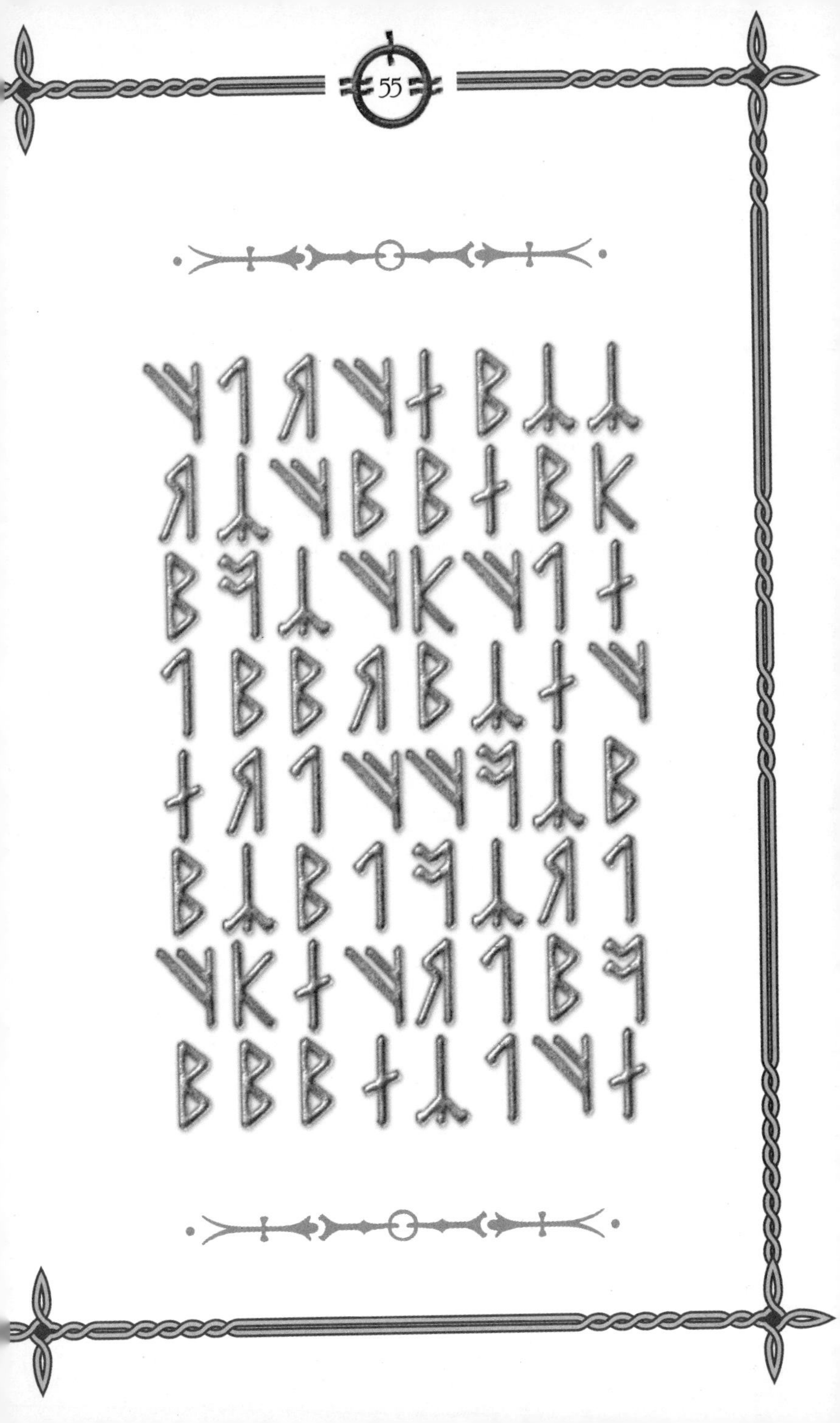

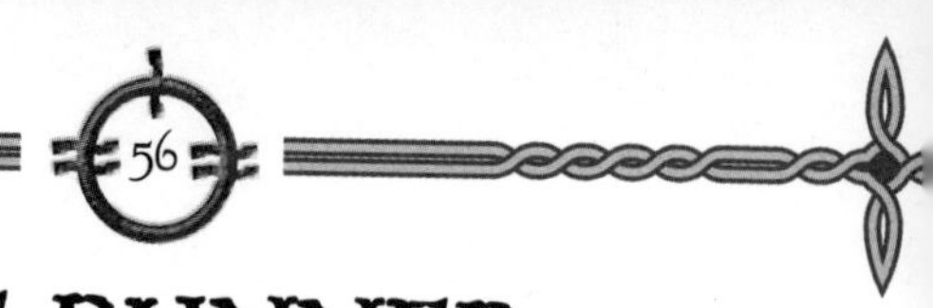

THE RUNNER

From the Great Green Book:

I run through woods and fields all day,
Sit under the bed at night in company,
With my long tongue hanging out,
Waiting only to be fed.

Who am I?

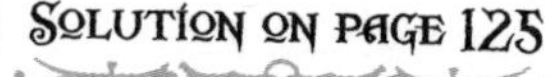

Solution on page 125

GORBAZ

"Damn that Boldog," Gorbaz muttered. "A third his age! I'll lead my own patrol before then and damn his filthy hide. Even if I have to cut it out of his gullet. I'm twenty-two, damn him, and he's only fifty-eight years more 'n me. Fah, he's nothing. Damn him."

"What's that, stinky?" Boldog looked irritated.

"Nothing," said Gorbaz sullenly.

How long does Gorbaz have to wait?

SOLUTION ON PAGE 125

NUMENOR

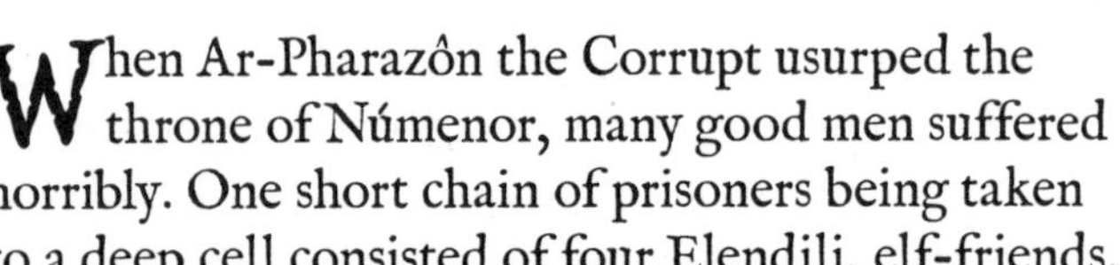

When Ar-Pharazôn the Corrupt usurped the throne of Númenor, many good men suffered horribly. One short chain of prisoners being taken to a deep cell consisted of four Elendili, elf-friends, each man tied to the one behind him, like a snake.

Indilzar was fastened to Nimruz, but not to Belzagar. Belzagar was not chained to Abattar. So who was?

SOLUTION ON PAGE 125

FORTUNE

A generous soul, favoured by fortune, decided to do what he could to help his fellow men. Each week, he assembled a stack of one pound grain-bags, and split them up evenly amongst the needy who came to him for aid. On one particular week, he calculated that if five less people had approached him, each share would have been two bags greater; instead, four extra people appealed for help, and the share was one bag less.

How many bags of grain did he give away each week?

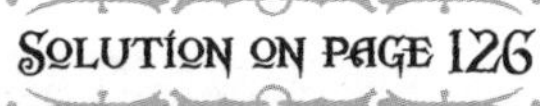
SOLUTION ON PAGE 126

THE BLIND

From the Great Green Book:

Here, here, here, he says, and he tells true – but he has no eyes.

Who is he?

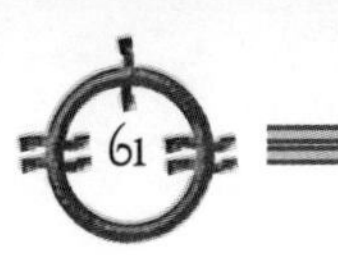

IN THE SHIRE

According to an engraving on an old tomb outside Frogmorton, inside are housed two grandmothers with their two granddaughters, two husbands with their two wives, two fathers with their two daughters, two mothers with their two sons, two maids with their two mothers, and two sisters with their two elder brothers. Despite this, only six names are listed. How can this be?

SOLUTIONS ON PAGE 126

ESCAPE

Fleeing from enemies, three companions find themselves with just one horse. The steed can carry a rider plus a passenger, and moves at 8 leagues an hour, while the healthy walker can manage 2 leagues an hour, and the third, who is slightly wounded, just 1 league an hour. Their destination is 40 leagues away, and they resolve to arrive simultaneously.

How quickly can they get there?

SOLUTION ON PAGE 127

WELL

From the Great Green Book:

A deep well is ringed with chisels.
Thus do I speak true – and false.

What is it?

Solution on page 127

MENAGERIE

As they crossed the plains of Gorgoroth, Frodo and Sam saw many strange and horrible things. One morning, they saw an orc push past with a team of vile beasts, as if they were cattle. Some of the creatures were biped, like massive birds, and the others quadruped, corrupted beasts. While Frodo counted thirty-six heads, Sam noticed one hundred feet. But he also maintained that two of the birds had somehow come to possess four feet, not two.

How many birds and beasts were there?

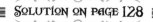

SOLUTION ON PAGE 128

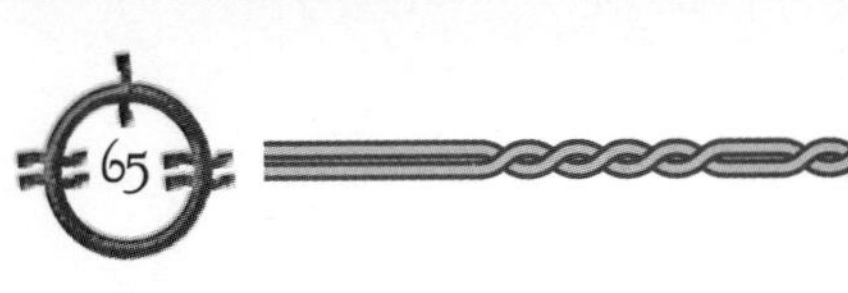

STILL

From the Great Green Book:

Two bodies have I,
Though both joined in one
The stiller I stand,
The faster I run.

Who am I?

Solution on page 128

ELFSTONE

Elessar Telcontar, King of Gondor and Arnor - known as Aragorn son of Arathorn - was as wise as he was mighty. A few years into his rule, a carpenter was killed in a drunken Minas Tirith brawl. The other participants in the fight were rounded up, sobered out, and brought before the King to find the truth.

"Felegorn, you killed that poor man," said Cirithor.

"He may have, but I most certainly did not," Aromir said.

Turgondir shook his head. "Well, Hallas is definitely not the one to blame."

Felegorn scowled at Cirithor. "Cirithor lies, he can't help it, and he doesn't like me."

"Be that as it may," said Hallas, "Aromir is telling the truth."

Just two of the men dared lie, as King Elessar quickly noted. Who struck the fatal blow?

SOLUTION ON PAGE 128

THINGS

From the Great Green Book:

There are two hairy things, and it's pleasant to have them meet.

What are they?

Solution on page 129

SCOUTS

Four small bands of scouts were tasked with infiltrating Mirkwood in search of information. Members of each group were given coloured bands to wear around their forearms, as aids to identification in the dismal forest. The four groups were trackers, climbers, sneakers and spotters.

The trackers wore neither red nor yellow bands.
The climbers wore neither yellow nor white bands.
The sneakers wore neither white nor red bands.
The spotters wore neither yellow nor red bands.
Furthermore, someone wore blue bands, and if the trackers were not white, then the climbers were not red.

What colour was assigned to which group?

SOLUTION ON PAGE 129

VICTIM

From the Great Green Book:

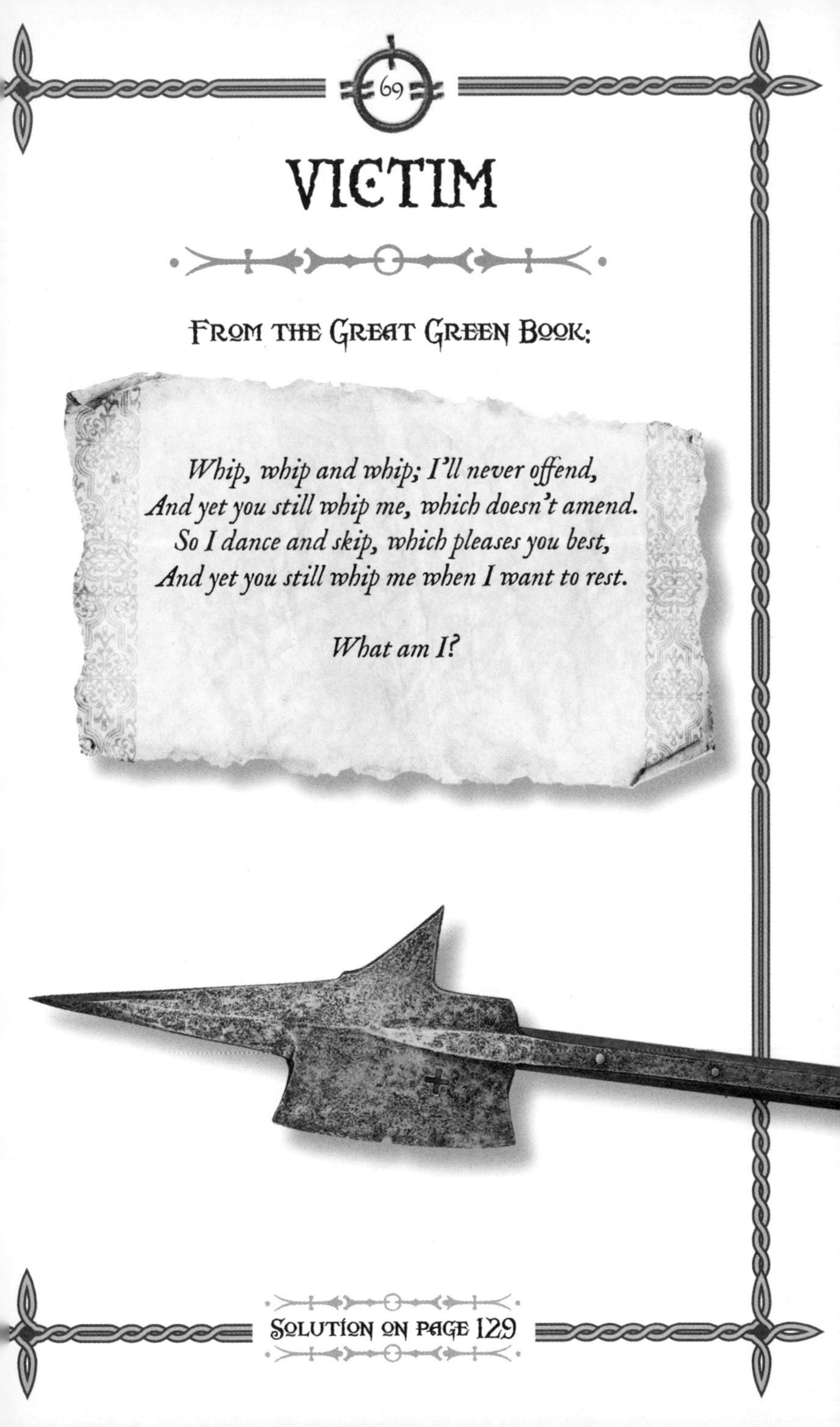

Whip, whip and whip; I'll never offend,
And yet you still whip me, which doesn't amend.
So I dance and skip, which pleases you best,
And yet you still whip me when I want to rest.

What am I?

Solution on page 129

INNOCENCE

From the Great Green Book:

Sign of youth and innocence,
Enclosed with walls for my defence,
I boldly spread my charms around,
'Till some rude lover twists me round,
And at his breast I soon decay,
My beauty lost, I'm turned away.

Who am I?

Solution on page 130

RIDING FORTH

"So there I was, down in the East-fold, trapped up against the mountains in a small valley. I had bare rock behind me, and forty orcs in front. Rather than rush in, and face my blade, one of the filthy scum hit upon the idea of roast Eorlingas for dinner. The wind was in their favour, so they set fire to the long grass all along the valley's opening and waited for me to burn."

"The fact you're standing here to make that boast names you a liar, Éomer."

"Don't be a fool, Háma. It was a dire situation, but not fatal. I couldn't climb to safety or find shelter from the flame, but I was hardly helpless."

"So how did you avoid the fire, then?"

What do you think?

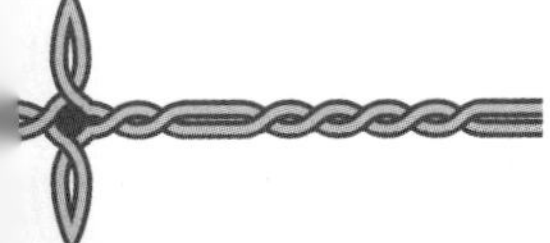

SOLUTION ON PAGE 130

SPEAR-NOSE

Feggi and Nefgeirr of Esgaroth fought mightily in the Battle of the Five Armies. Grandfather and grandson, it was thought amongst the Lake-towners that the one was too young to survive the battle, and the other too old. And yet they covered themselves in gore and glory, and returned home triumphant. Forty-four years was the difference in their ages, and 1,280 the total obtained by multiplying them together.

How old were they?

SOLUTION ON PAGE 131

WOOL

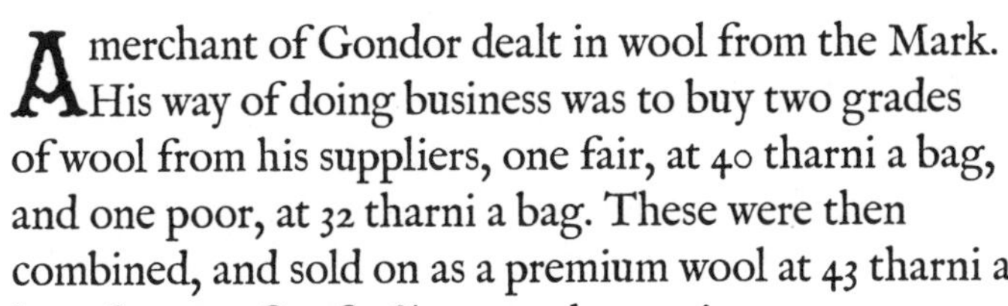

A merchant of Gondor dealt in wool from the Mark. His way of doing business was to buy two grades of wool from his suppliers, one fair, at 40 tharni a bag, and one poor, at 32 tharni a bag. These were then combined, and sold on as a premium wool at 43 tharni a bag, for a profit of 25% on purchase price.

What is the ratio of the 'premium' mix?

SOLUTION ON PAGE 131

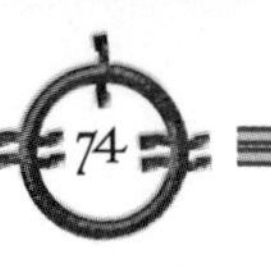

WOSES

A patriarch of the Drúedain claimed, while guiding a pack of Rohirrim warriors through Drúadan Forest, to be amongst the most profligate of his peoples. He placed his age in years at something between 50 and 80. Each of his sons, he claimed, had as many sons as brothers, and the old man had one son or grandson for each year of his life.

How old was he?

Solution on page 131

COMFORT

From the Great Green Book:

What is it that sleeps with its head down?

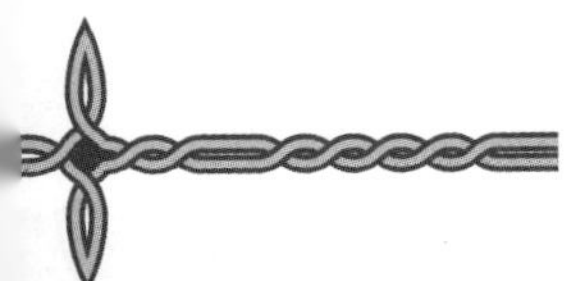

Solution on page 132

FUN AND GAMES

"Let us play a game," the dragon said. "If you do well, I may delay eating you."

The dwarf shuddered. "As you will," he said grimly.

"Capital. Imagine that you have a pair of buckets, one half the size of the other. Next, imagine filling the smaller one half-way with oil, and the larger one to the one-third mark. Then, fill both buckets to the brim with water, and pour them both into an empty barrel. What is the proportion of oil to water in the barrel?"

SOLUTION ON PAGE 132

PRINCESS

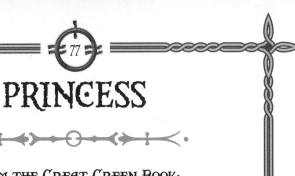

From the Great Green Book:

There are two bewitching princesses,
who live on two sides of a mountain.
When one cries, they both cry.

Who are they?

Solution on page 133

COLUMN

A column of archers are advancing through a valley. A messenger, sent from the rear of the column to the front, takes 140 yard-long strides to get there. His return requires just 20 strides. Can you tell the length of the column?

SOLUTION ON PAGE 133

WOOLLY THINKING

Four shepherds of the Vale gathered one lunchtime where their pastures met, and soon fell to discussing their flocks. After some debate, they decided that since Calder had ten more sheep than Da, if Calder gave a quarter of his sheep to Balder, then he and Audun together would have as many sheep as Balder and Da. Furthermore, if Audun then gave one third of his sheep to Balder, who in turn passed a quarter of his new flock to Calder, who likewise gave a fifth of his sheep to Da - and, finally, Balder gave a quarter of his sheep to be divided equally amongst the other three - then they'd all have the same number of sheep.

How many sheep did each man have?

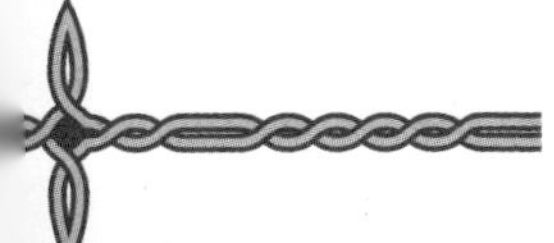

SOLUTION ON PAGE 133

THE TABLE

"Fool. I could transport you this very instant to the centre of a table so vast and so perfectly smooth and without friction, that you'd be unable to move upon it. Every single motion you made would slip, without the slightest purchase. You would be stranded there for ever."

"I may not have magic at my call, but I'd escape your damned table, even if you dumped me there in just my underclothes."

How?

Solution on page 134

THE TWINS

FROM THE GREAT GREEN BOOK:

Two twins we are, and let it not surprise,
Alike in every feature, shape, and size.
We make ourselves of use, and for our pains,
We by the neck are often hung in chains.

What are we?

SOLUTION ON PAGE 134

GONDOR

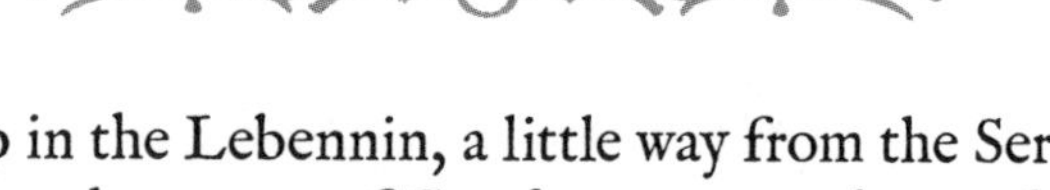

Deep in the Lebennin, a little way from the Serni river, three men of Gondor met together under the cover of night. Their purpose was as dark as their surroundings, and fell deeds were plotted before the conspirators separated to return to their unobtrusive lives in Arnach, Linhir and Minas Brethil.

The meeting place they chose, distinguished by a weathered menhir, was equally as far from each of the three towns. If I tell you that it is 30 leagues from Arnach to Minas Brethil, 28 leagues from Minas Brethis to Linhir, and 26 leagues from Linhir to Arnach, then how far is the meeting space from the town?

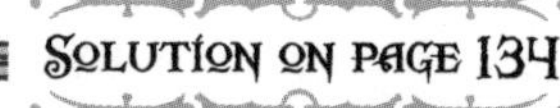
Solution on page 134

THE FIRST

From the Great Green Book:

Before the elves arose, my early days began.
I ape each creature, and resemble man.
I gently creep o'er the tops of tender grass,
Nor leave the least impression where I pass.
Touch me you may, but I can ne'er be felt,
Nor ever yet was tasted, heard, or smelt,
Yet seen each day – if not, be sure at night
You'll quickly find me out by candlelight.

What am I?

Solution on page 135

INDEED

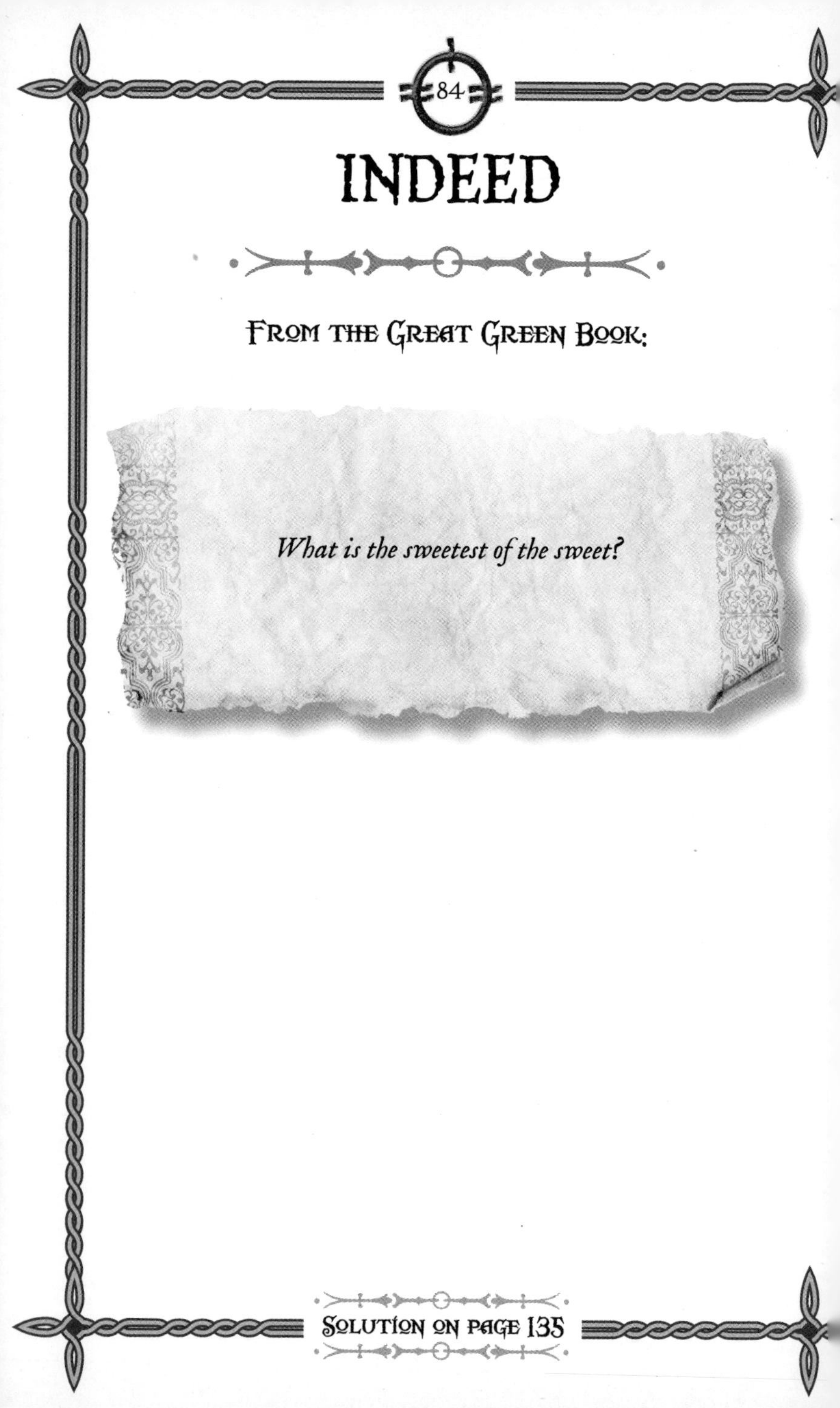

From the Great Green Book:

What is the sweetest of the sweet?

Solution on page 135

HARADRIM

A group of Haradrim soldiers were squabbling over a broken tablet. Each was anxious to avoid the wrath of their stern sergeant, and of the three statements each made, one was a lie.

Herumor said, "It wasn't me. I've never shattered anything. Mummakan did it."
Sangahyando said, "I am innocent. Fuinur is guilty. I have known Dalamir for years."
Fuinur said, "I didn't do it. Neither did Dalamir. Sangahyando hates me."
Dalamir said, "I am innocent. I don't even know Sangahyando. Mummakan is guilty."
Mummakan said, "I am not guilty. Sangahyando is the one. Herumor lied about me."

Which man is to blame?

Solution on page 135

THE CIRTH 3

Dwarfish rune-boards were commonly encoded with junk information to make translation difficult. Before proper decoding could begin, it was necessary to remove the extra runes. This was accomplished by ensuring that each column and row had no more than one instance of any given runic symbol. Extra runes had to be deleted from each column and row, with the extra rules that no two deleted runes could be horizontally or vertically adjacent, and that the main, undeleted runes had to form one single sprawling group of horizontally and/or vertically touching runes.

Can you remove the junk information from this board?

SOLUTION ON PAGE 136

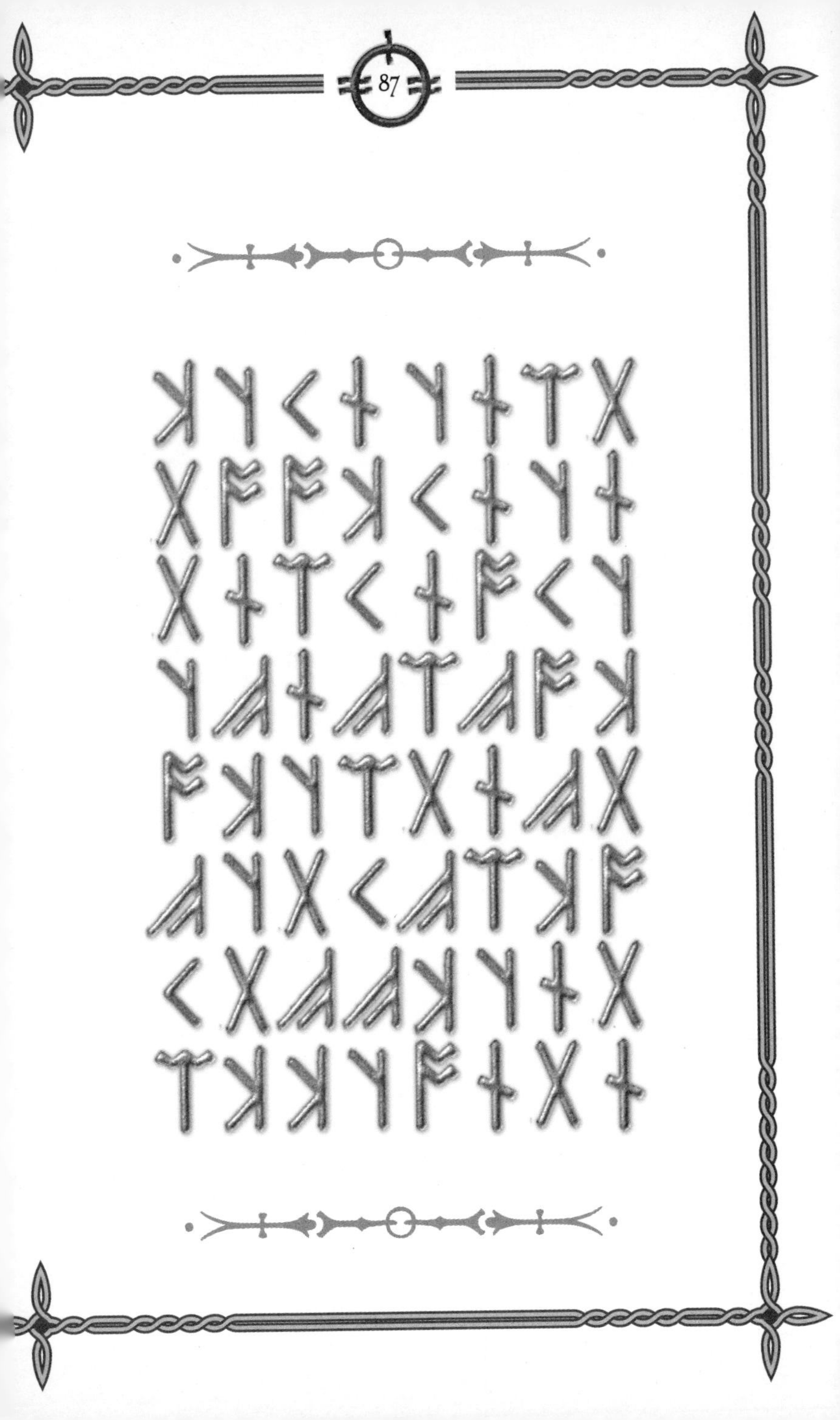

SIREN

From the Great Green Book:

It foams without anger,
It flies without wings,
It cuts without edge,
Without tongue it sings,
And yet do men dream of it.

What is it?

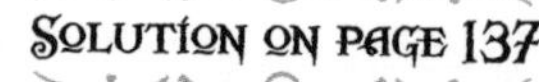

Solution on page 137

POST

As punishment for snoozing on the job, an unfortunate orc guard was ordered to march up and down along a row of posts. There were seven posts in the row, each two yards apart, and the instructions were to count each post in turn, up and down - counting the first and last just once, not twice - until he had counted a thousand posts. If he failed to identify that post correctly, he would be forced to start again, counting to two thousand.

Which post is the thousandth?

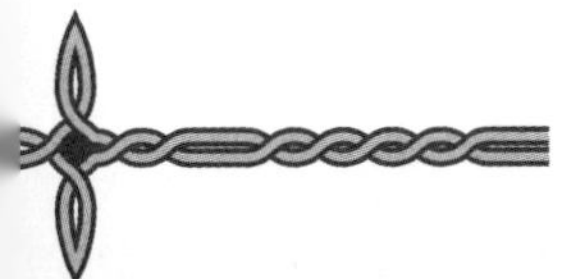

SOLUTION ON PAGE 137

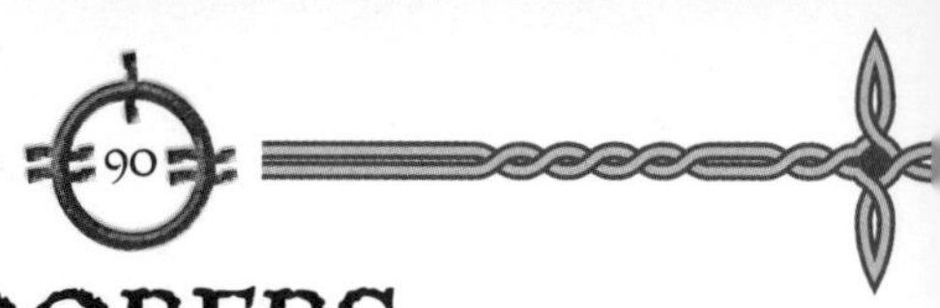

COOPERS

It was well known, amongst the craftsfolk of Minas Tirith that Orodlas's sons were fine coopers, but took their time over their work. Together, Egalmoth and Faren could turn out twenty-five barrels in eight days. Egalmoth and Pelemir together could do it in nine days, and Faren and Pelemir would take ten days. Needless to say, Pelemir was not especially popular, but how long would it take him to do fifty barrels on his own, with neither of his brothers helping?

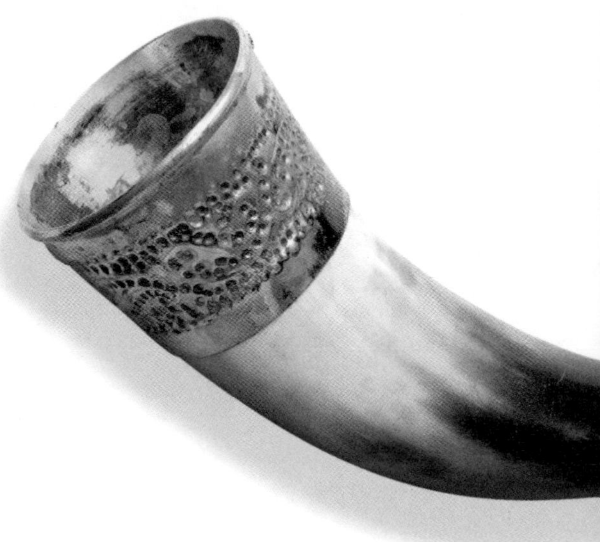

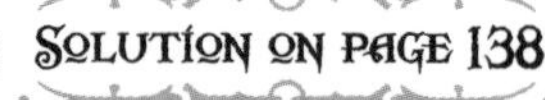

SOLUTION ON PAGE 138

SPITE

From the Great Green Book:

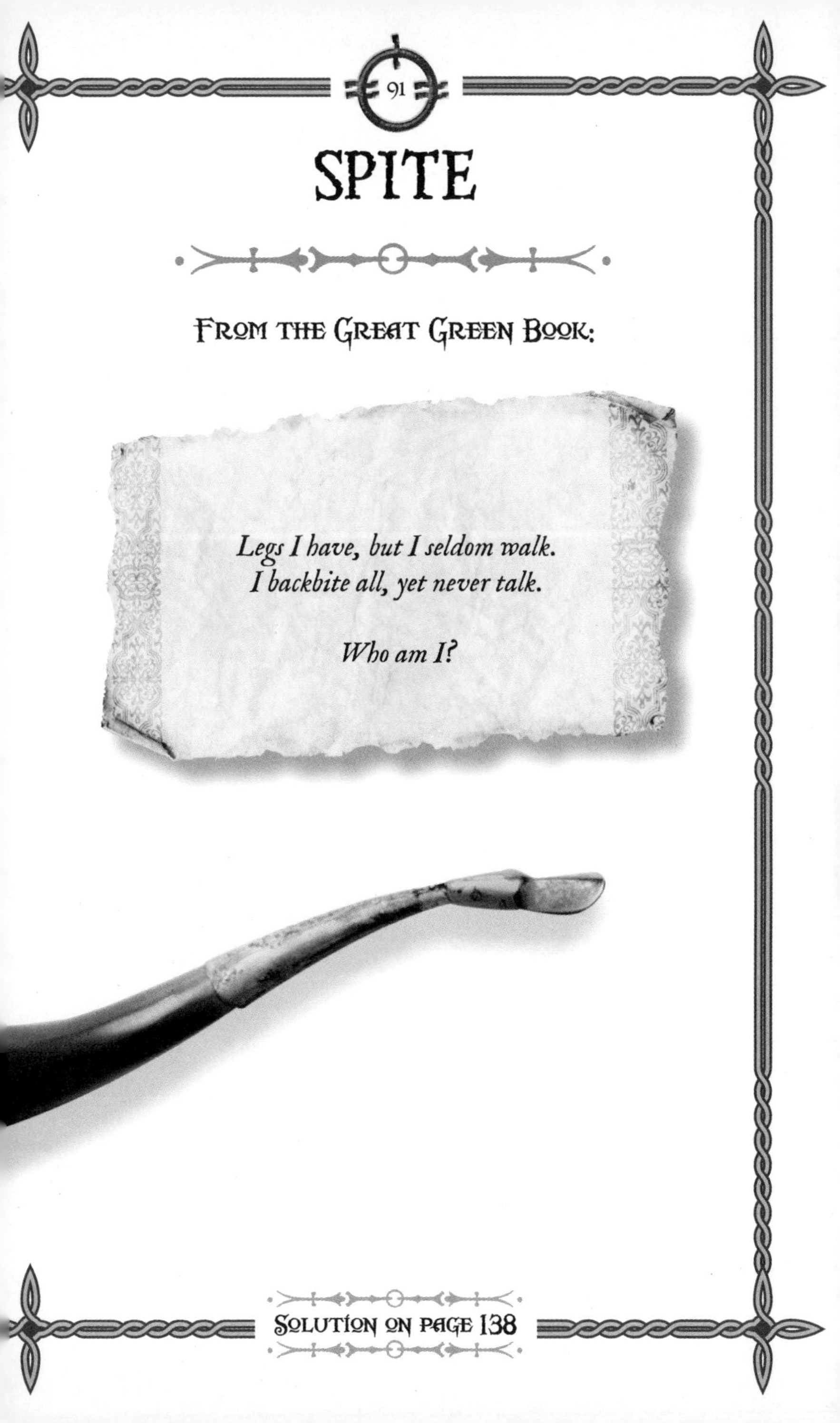

Legs I have, but I seldom walk.
I backbite all, yet never talk.

Who am I?

Solution on page 138

THE NINE

Nine travellers were on an urgent journey. As the afternoon wore on, the destination to their preferred resting place was still 20 miles, when they came across a carter. The man was happy to help, but his cart could only hold three men at one time. To minimise the journey, he offered to take them part-way in groups of three whilst the others continued walking, so that they would all reach their haven at the same time. The cart went at 20mph, while the travellers were able to keep a steady pace of 4mph.

With the carter's help, how long did it take to reach their destination?

SOLUTION ON PAGE 139

THE NINE REDUX

From the Great Green Book:

I saw nine birds.
I shot five of them.

How many were left?

Solution on page 139

ANGMAR

In the middle of the Third Age, as the Witch-King of Angmar prepared his final campaign against Fornost, the dungeons of his capital city, Carn Dûm, grew crowded with conscripts and camp assistants of all ages and sexes. Before the 'recruitment' push started, there were just 250 prisoners incarcerated in Carn Dûm, both male and female. A year later, eight times as many were locked up, and the women's numbers had grown three times as fast as the men's.

How many of each sex were there at the start of the drive?

SOLUTION ON PAGE 140

CHOPPER

"I once watched a man divide a huge pile of firewood into precisely ten stacks of 20lbs each, with none left over. He had a huge scale and two massive weights, 50lbs and 90lbs, to help him, though how he lifted the damned things is beyond me. And he did it all in just nine weighings!"

How was it done?

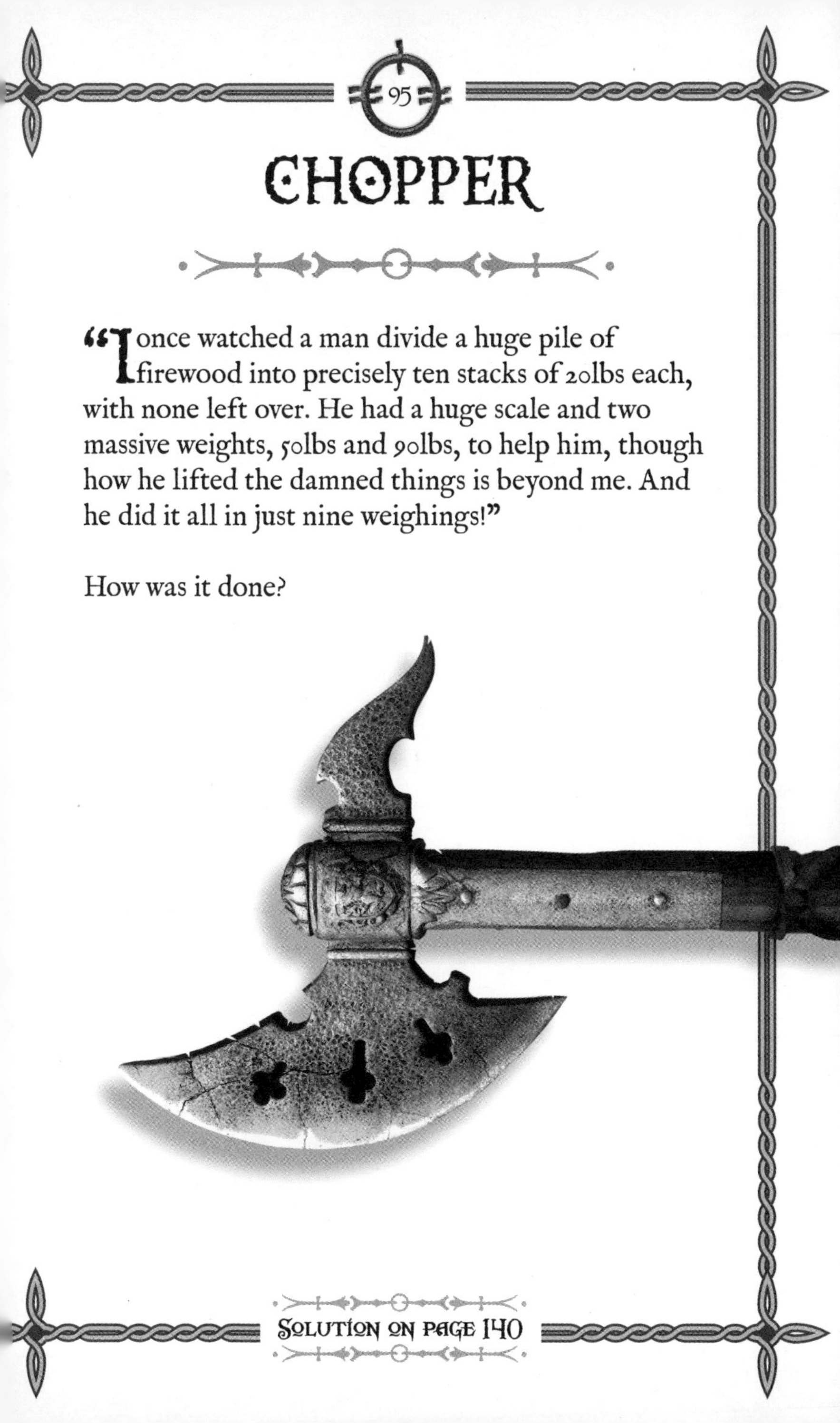

Solution on page 140

DUNGEONS

In the great fortress of Barad Eithel, the corridor to the dungeon was cunningly warded. Five great doors stood along its length, each on an independent cycle. The first opened every 1 minute and 45 seconds, the second every 1 minute and 10 seconds, the third every 2 minutes and 55 seconds, the fourth every 2 minutes and 20, and the last every 35 seconds. Each remained open for 10 seconds. All five opened at the same moment 12 times in every 7 hours, such moments always being closely watched by the jailer. Even at a flat sprint, the doors were 20 seconds apart, and if a cell was opened without a lever being thrown in the jailer's room within 2-and-a-half minutes, alarms would sound and the doors would all slam shut.

Was it possible to escape the corridor, and if so, at what point in the cycle would the prisoner have to flee the cell?

SOLUTION ON PAGE 141

BUNCE

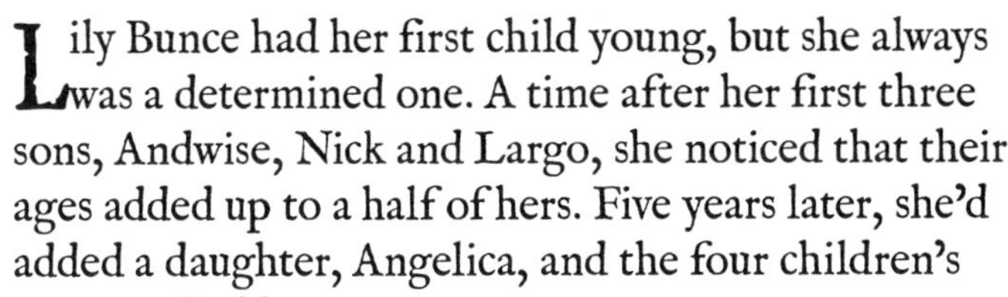

Lily Bunce had her first child young, but she always was a determined one. A time after her first three sons, Andwise, Nick and Largo, she noticed that their ages added up to a half of hers. Five years later, she'd added a daughter, Angelica, and the four children's ages totalled her own.

Ten more years after that, she'd had only one more child, Dora. Andwise and Dora together were as old as Largo and Angelica combined, and the five together were twice their mother's age. The eldest two children together, in fact, matched their mother's age precisely, and Andwise alone was as old as his sisters together.

How old are the Bunces?

Solution on page 141

THE BALROG'S CURSE

From the Great Green Book:

At least one of these statements is a lie.
At least two of these ten statements are lies.
At least three of these ten statements are lies.
At least four of these ten statements are lies.
At least five of these ten statements are lies.
At least six of these ten statements are lies.
At least seven of these ten statements are lies.
At least eight of these ten statements are lies.
At least nine of these ten statements are lies.
All ten of these ten statements are lies.

Which of the ten statements are lies?

Solutions on page 142

CONFIDENCE

From the Great Green Book:

I never was, am always to be,
No-one has ever or will yet meet me,
But I am the confidence of all
Who live and breathe on our spinning ball.

Who am I?

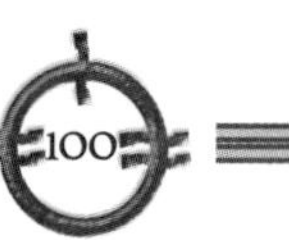

THE HOST

As the forces of Sauron advanced towards the Pelennor Fields, a scout of the Mark managed to get a count of the disposition of one of the great orc-hosts. At just over 21,000 warriors, it was split into five legions and great companies, each led by an orc-captain.

The scout estimated that a third of the first legion held as many foes as two sevenths of the second legion, seven twelfths of the third, nine thirteenths of the fourth, and fifteen twenty-secondths of the fifth.

How many orcs were there in each legion?

SOLUTION ON PAGE 143

CREATURE

From the Great Green Book:

I have a creature, a very strange creature.
Its body is hard, and its tooth is sharp.
It will not eat unless I strike its head.
When I do, it will consume even stone.

What is it?

Solution on page 143

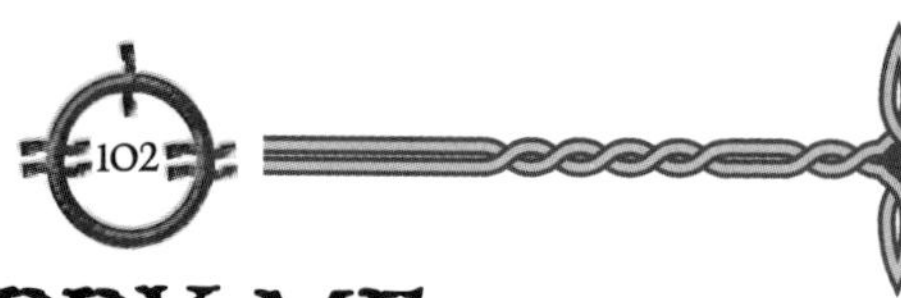

CARRY ME

From the Great Green Book:

I saw two boats go by, but only one person was on board.
"Carry me," they cried, "and I will carry you. Let us share alike."

What are they?

Solution on page 144

BURDENS

As the people of Rohan were preparing their retreat to Helm's Deep, it was decided that each kind of beast should take a different kind of liquid. What is known for sure is somewhat tangled. If donkeys carried wine, horses took oil, while if donkeys carried oil, the mules took wine. If horses took the wine however, the mules held oil.

Is there an animal whose load we know?

Solution on page 144

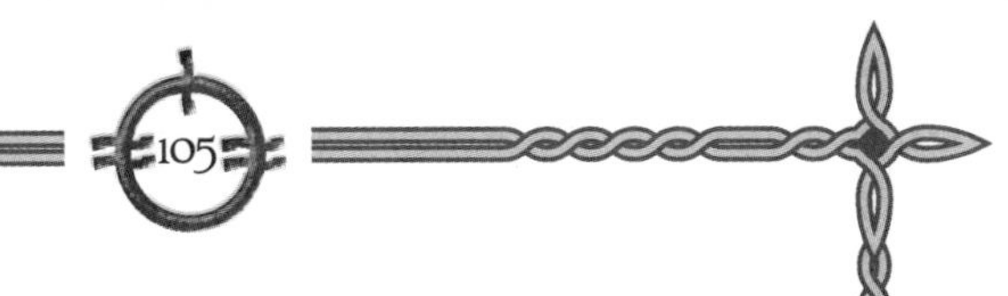

SOLUTIONS

"All that is gold does not glitter, not all those who wander are lost; the old that is strong does not wither, deep roots are not reached by the frost."

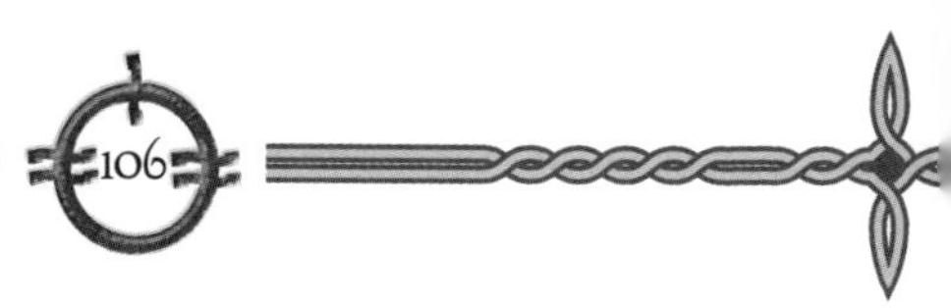

THE GREAT GREEN BOOK OF BUCKLAND

I am a candle. This is your warning, now; do not read much, if anything, into the titles of subsequent puzzles from the Great Green Book.

UNCERTAINTY

Today, which (yesterday) was tomorrow, and (tomorrow) will be yesterday.

GREATNESS

Alatar and Olorin's statements are mutually exclusive, so one of them must be telling the truth. That means Curomo is lying, and he - Saruman, in the Westron tongue of men - is the mightiest of the five.

FIVE ARMIES

In fact Nori did do best overall of the three.

For rapidity, Dori to Bofur is 5:2, and Dori to Nori is 3:4 - or 20:15:6 for Nori, Dori and Bofur in order.

Number of blows needed gives Nori 5:1 over Dori and 3:5 to Bofur, or 15:3:25 in the same order as lightness.

Strength of foes tells us that Bofur's enemies were four times as strong as Nori's, and Dori's are three times as tough again, so the ratio is 1:12:4 in order.

Totalling those scores, we get 36 for Nori, 30 for Dori and 35 for Bofur.

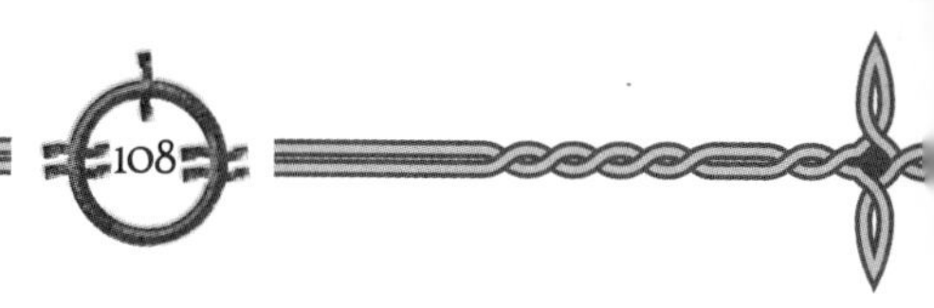

RACE

No. The larger animal will catch the smaller one after 240 seconds, having run approximately 2880 feet.

THE BEAST

A quill-pen.

GAMWICH

Pick up the signpost and point the Hobbiton sign back the way you'd just come. Then all the other signs would be pointing in the right direction too.

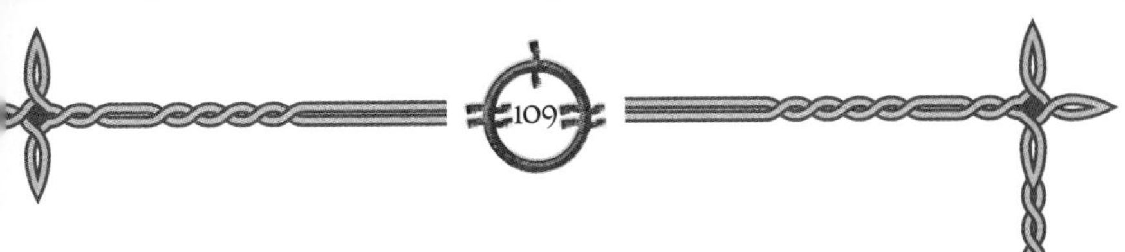

MAD BAGS

Compound interest of 50% for 18 years, starting from 200 farthings, would return 295,578.38 farthings.

AFTERMATH

Just one. All three dwarves have the wrong pack so if Bofur has Dori's pack, Dori must have Nori's pack, and Nori must have Bofur's pack - for if Bofur has Dori's pack and Dori has Bofur's, then Nori would have the correct pack. The same principle holds true for Bofur having Nori's pack.

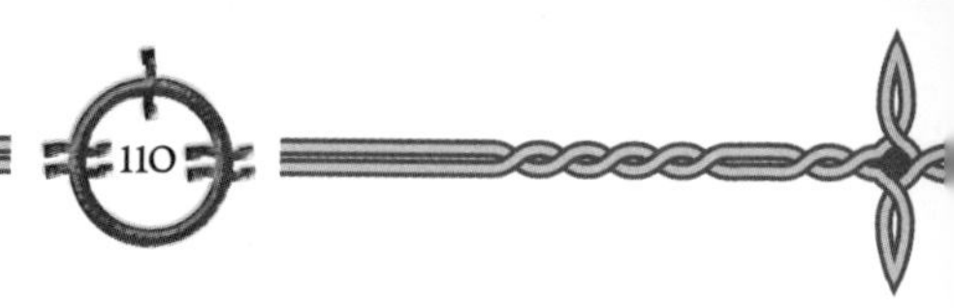

BYWATER

Hob is a simpleton, Tod has a temper, Bom is a drunkard, and Ron is a know-it-all ... alternately Bom is a simpleton, Tod a know-it-all, Hob has a temper and Ron is a drunkard!

THE MARTYR

A mortar bowl.

THE STAND

My heel (assuming I step in a forward direction).

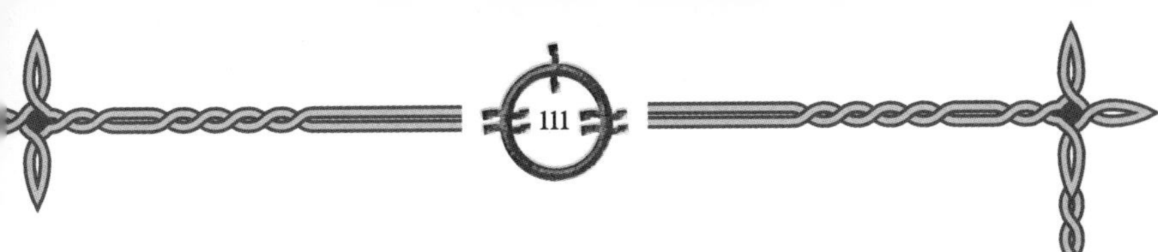

FAMILY TIES

Second cousin twice removed.

DEPLOYMENT

There are 1023 elvish fighters. The only way to be able to guarantee any arbitrary number of that amount or less is through geometric progression - so the deployment is as units containing 1, 2, 4, 8, 16, 32, 64, 128, 256 and 512 elves.

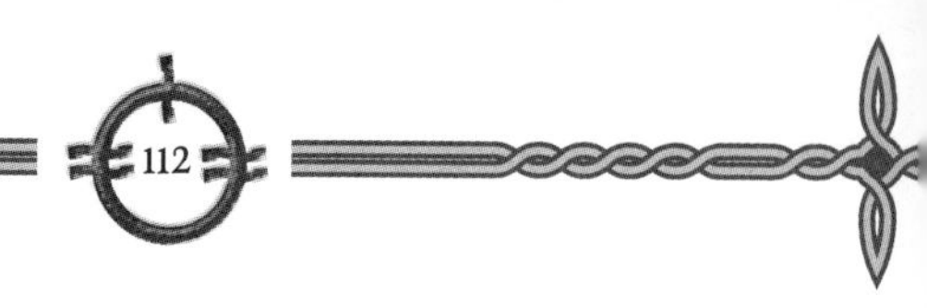

BANDO

Seven plums. Since a peach is worth six plums and an apple, then that plus three apples matches ten plums, and plums and apples weigh the same.

MILD

Neither. Both pitchers hold the same amount of liquid before and after the operation. Since no liquid has been lost, however much mild there is in the dark, there also has to be exactly the same amount of dark in the mild.

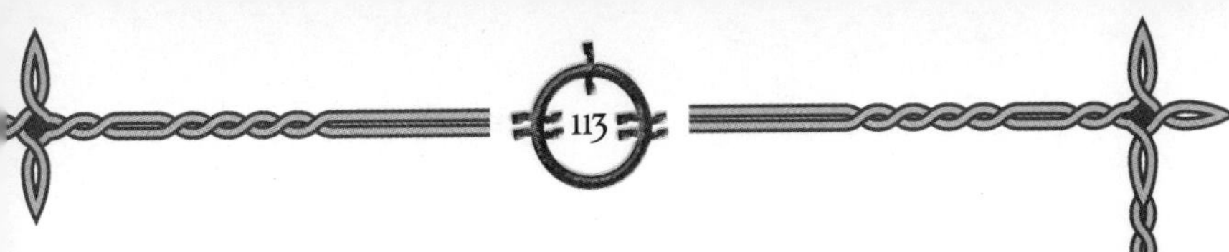

COMPANIONS

The four cardinal directions, north, east, south and west.

AGE

108. If $x/6 + x/4 + x/2 + 9 = x$, then $11x/12 + 9 = x$, and $x = 9*12$.

GOLDSPINE

Ask a question to which the answer has to be yes, such as "Are you Troga Goldspine?"

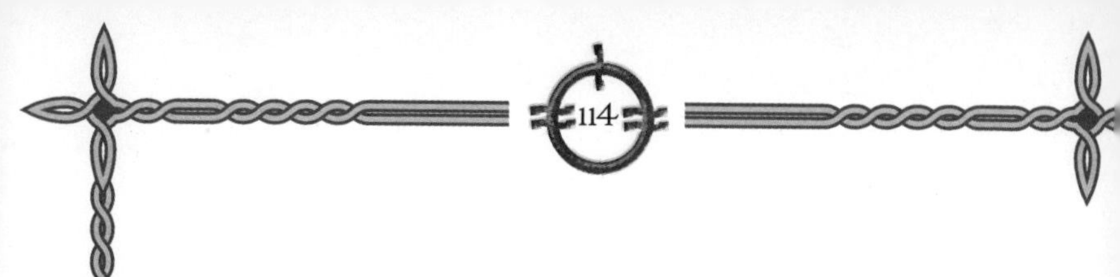

VITALITY

A hole.

THE SINGER

A drum.

INTRUDER

His wife had just given birth to their baby.

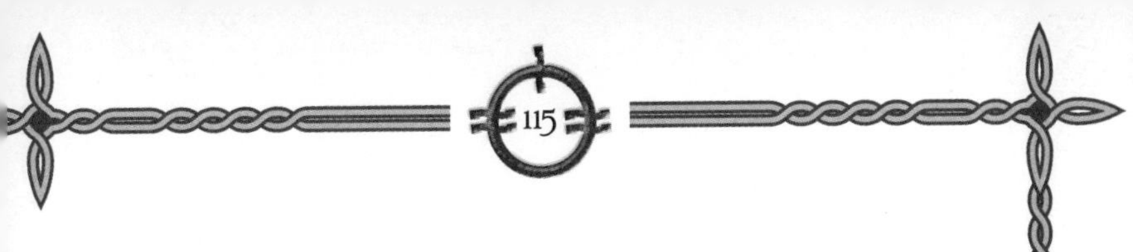

MORIA

83. Start by figuring out the most slates needed at once for each number. For '1', this would be 111 plus three other numbers with two 11s in - that's nine slates. 0 is different, having no possible triple, so just eight slates will do. No nines are needed, as sixes can be reversed, but four numbers consisting entirely of 6s and 9s could happen, so there have to be twelve 6s. So then, 8+9+9+9+9+9+12+9+9+0=83.

GIFTS

A coffin.

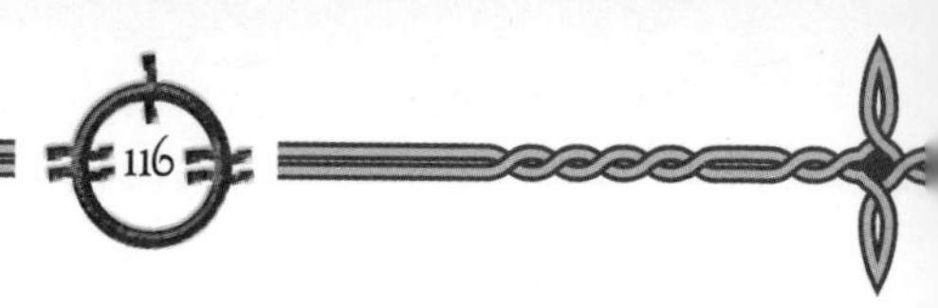

COMMUNIQUE

Five out of six messages will arrive,
and of those, five out of six replies will arrive.
So the chance is 25/36, or 69.4%.

CROOKED

A key.

WILL

The secret number is 36. So, in decreasing order, the bequests are 1296, 72, 38, 36, 34, 18 and 6 gold pieces.

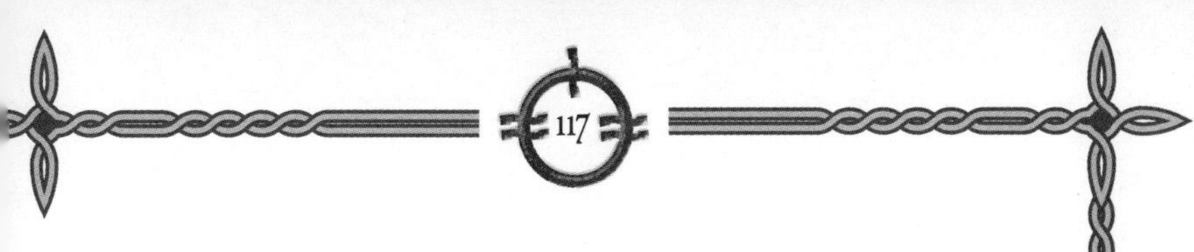

TRAITOR

It's Sirion. If Anardil is the murderer, all we can know is that Castagir is in the upper gardens. If Castagir is the murderer, we can deduce nothing at all. But if Sirion is in the morning room, this places Castagir in the upper gardens, then Anardil in the feast hall, Ostoher in the great hall, Valacar in the grand balcony, and finally Tarond in the library.

RUIN

Wine.

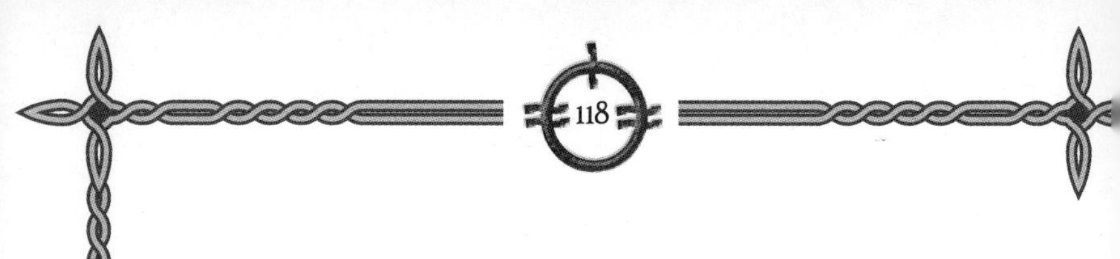

THE CIRTH 1

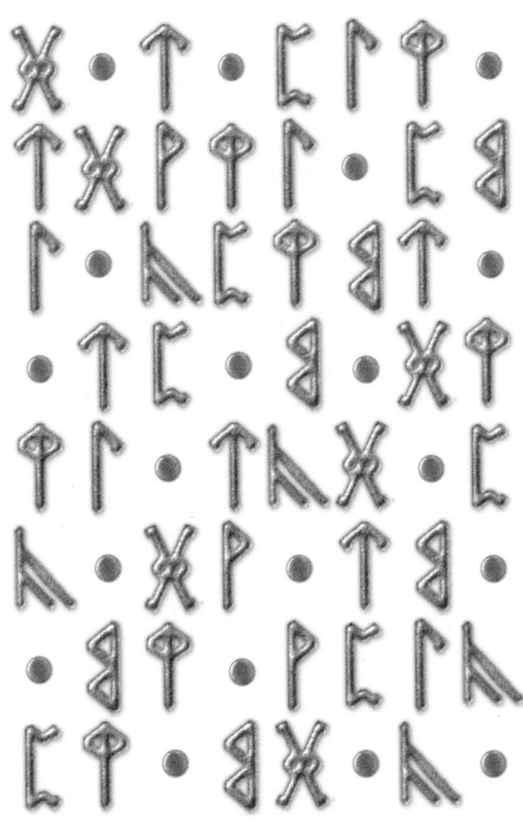

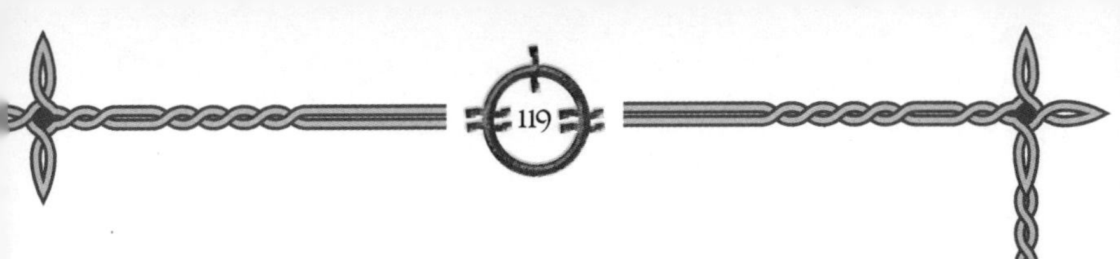

WINDOWS

The openings in the head - eyes, mouth, nostrils and earholes.

TWINS

Nori is on the right. Both twins will answer 'yes' to the question, but only the honest one can truthfully state what the other must say.

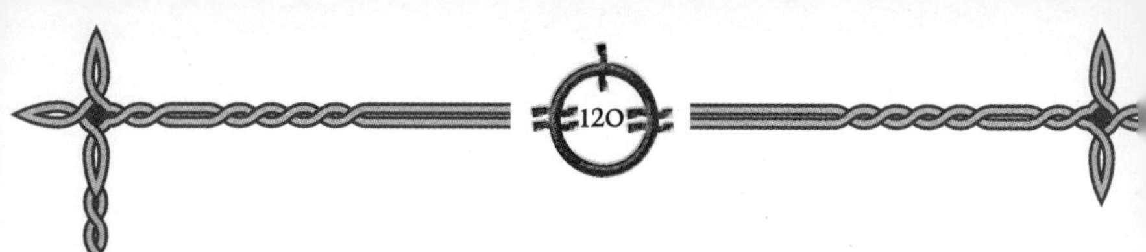

PURSUIT

Noon.

FORTH

Neither the honest man nor the liar can deny being truthful, so the first man is the unpredictable one. Similarly, the liar cannot deny being unpredictable, so the third man is the honest one, and the liar is the second one.

THE KEEP

A honeycomb.

THE RIDER

While the old man walks 52 paces, the rider travels the entire distance, which is 312+52 paces, or 364. 364/52 = 7, so the rider is travelling at 21 miles an hour.

THE WAY

Pains.

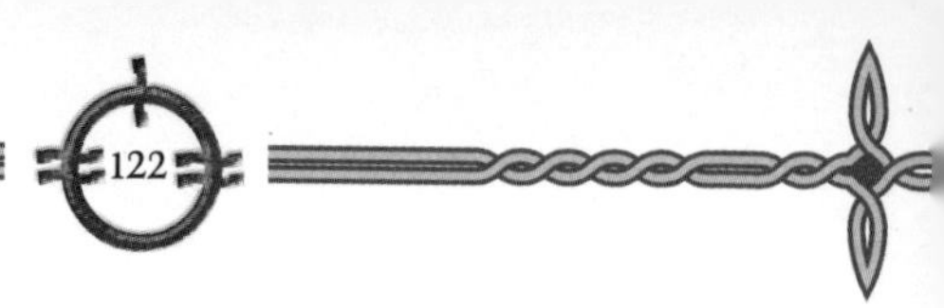

MARKET

Fram has 10 pigs and a horse, Ceorl has 6 cows and a horse, and Baldor has 20 sheep and a horse.

REDRUM

The smallest number that fits the bill is seven - a married couple, their three children (two female and one male) and the husband's parents.

SPREAD

An oil lamp.

THE GAMBLE

The sums are 105 shillings at 4-1, 84 shillings at 5-1, 70 shillings at 6-1 and 60 shillings at 7-1. We know 4a = 5b = 6c = 7d = a+b+c+d+101 = x. That means x has to have 4, 5, 6, and 7 as factors. From that we can easily find x=420, and dividing by 4, 5, 6, and 7 gives us the sums. 105+84+70+60+101 = 420.

CAPTIVITY

A pair of spurs.

THE CIRTH 2

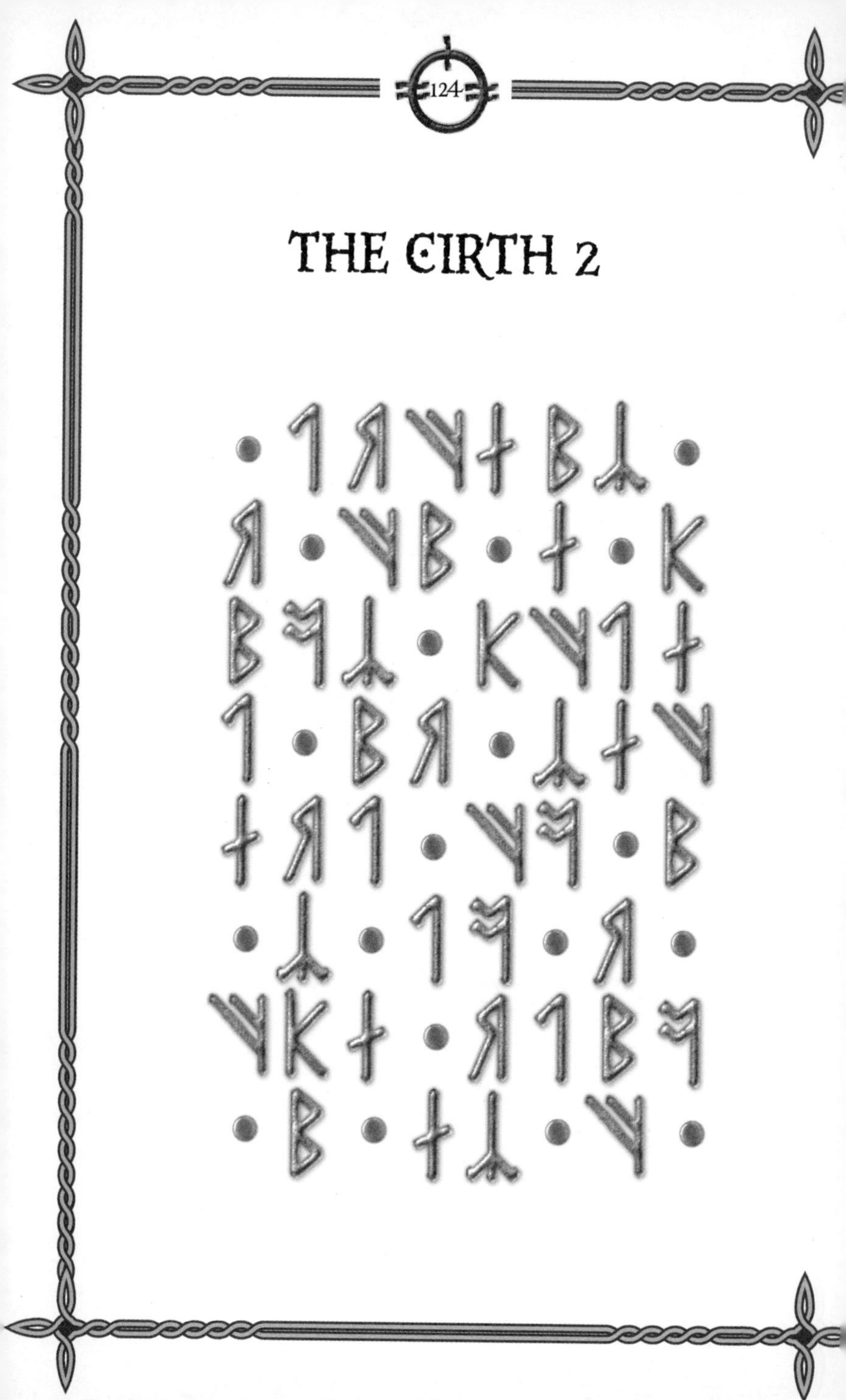

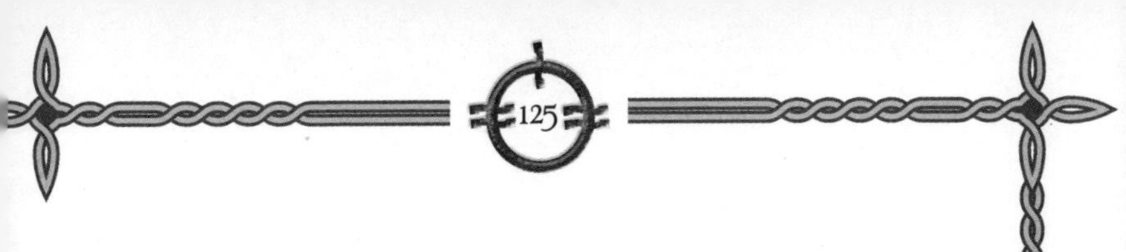

THE RUNNER

A shoe.

GORBAZ

Seven years. Then he will be 29, and Boldog 87.

NUMENOR

Indilzar. Since Belzagar cannot be linked to Indilzar or Abattar, he must be linked to Nimruz at one end of the chain. The only remaining space is to link to Indilzar, at the other end of the chain.

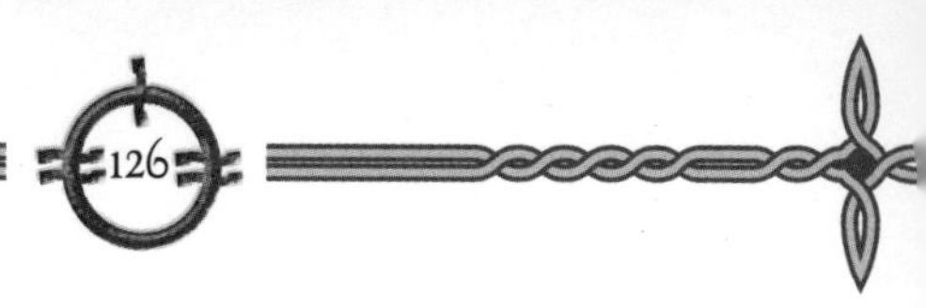

FORTUNE

120. With 20 regular applicants getting 6 bags each, five less would mean 15 people getting 8 bags, while four more would be 24 people getting 5 each.

THE BLIND

A pointing finger.

IN THE SHIRE

Two widows with adult sons each married the son of the other. Each new couple then had a daughter.

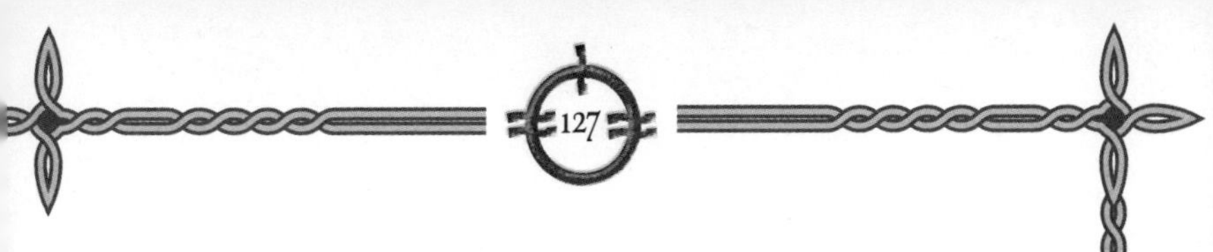

ESCAPE

In 10 hours, 7 minutes (and 12 seconds).
The slower walker must be carried first, and dropped off 5.85 leagues from the end, after 4.27 hours. By the time the rider has got back to the faster walker, slightly over 2.5 hours later, he will have walked 13.66 leagues over 6.83 hours, leaving 26.34 leagues to go in 3.29 hours.

WELL

A mouth.

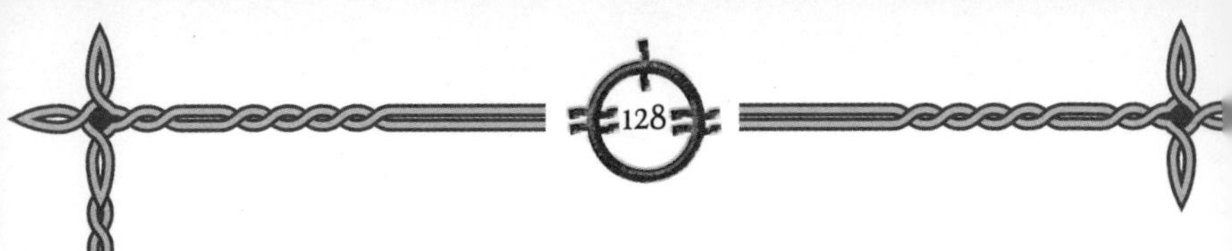

MENAGERIE

Allowing for the two odd birds adding four legs, 24 birds and 12 beasts.

STILL

An hourglass.

ELFSTONE

Hallas is guilty. Cirithor and Turgondir are the liars.

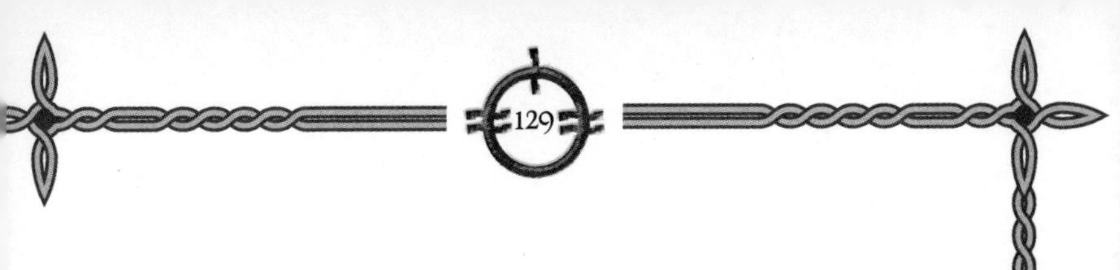

THINGS

Eyelids.

SCOUTS

The climbers must be red, which can only happen if the trackers are white. The spotters didn't wear yellow, so they must be blue, which leaves yellow for the sneakers.

VICTIM

A spinning-top.

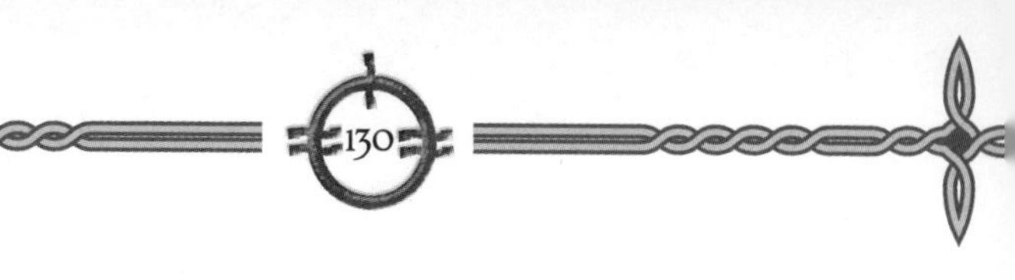

INNOCENCE

A rose.

RIDING FORTH

"I moved towards the middle of the valley, and set light to the area behind me, which then burned in the same direction as the orcs' fires. I then retreated into my own burnt spot, and as the orc-flames guttered around it, I mounted Fire-Foot and tore through the unsuspecting fools."

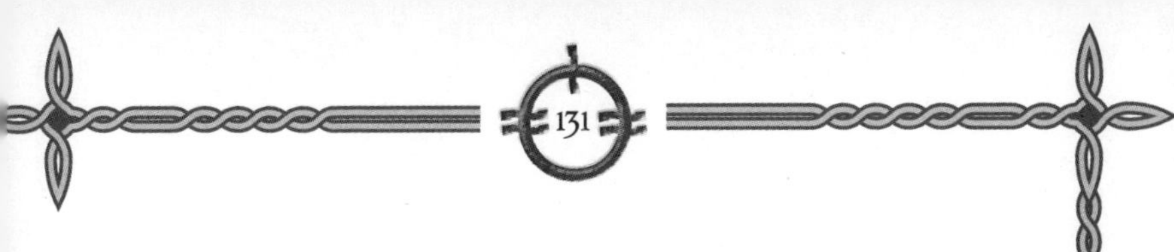

SPEAR-NOSE

Nefgeirr and Feggi are 20 and 64.

WOOL

If 43 tharni is a 25% profit, then the price of the mix must be 34.4 tharni, which means it is 70% poor wool and 30% fair wool.

WOSES

Sixty-four. He had eight sons,
each of which had produced seven further sons,
for a total of 56 grandsons.

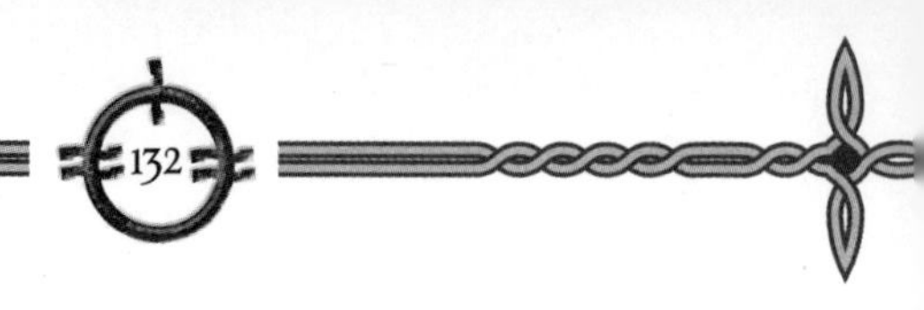

COMFORT

A bat.

FUN AND GAMES

7/18ths of oil to 11/18ths of water. From the larger bucket, a third of oil, and two thirds of water. From the smaller, effectively a quarter of oil and a quarter of water. Therefore we have a third plus a quarter of oil, and two thirds plus a quarter of water.

PRINCESS

The eyes.

COLUMN

35 yards. The column is x yards long, and for each stride the messenger takes, it walks y further, lengthening his journey. So y has to be less than a yard, or else the messenger would never get there, and $x + 140y = 140$. On the way back, similarly, $x - 20y = 20$. So $y = 120/160$, or three quarters of a yard, and $x = 35$ yards.

WOOLLY THINKING

There are 180 sheep in total. The even distribution at the end provides 45 sheep each, and Audun has 60, Balder 50, Calder 40 and Da 30.

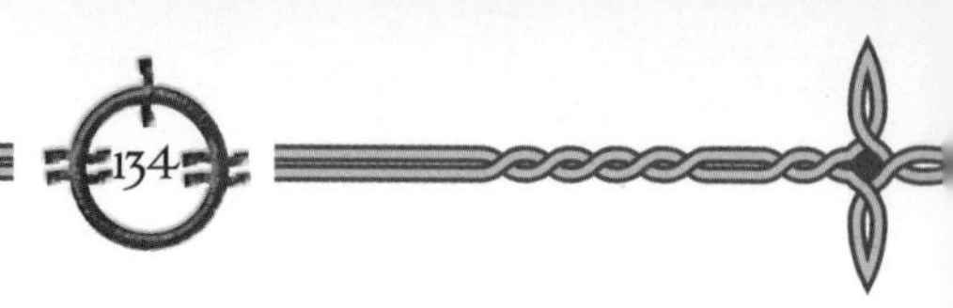

THE TABLE

By blowing. When you breathe in, air comes from every angle around your mouth, and produces very little force, but when you breathe out, the blast is focussed, particularly if you blow firmly. There's no friction to overcome, so you could slide yourself off the table with just your breath.

THE TWINS

A pair of scales.

GONDOR

Sixteen-and-a-quarter leagues.

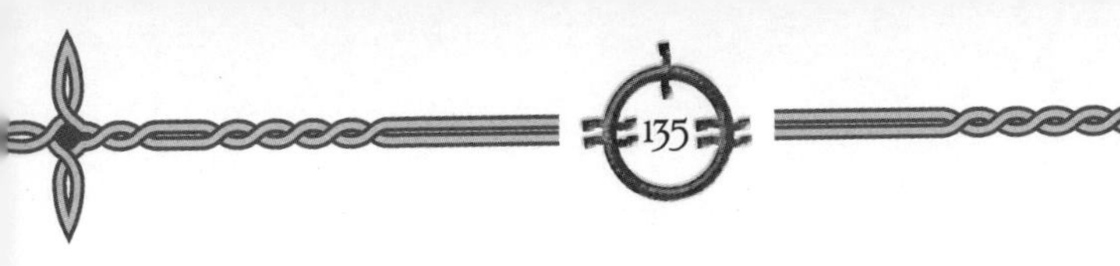

THE FIRST

Shadow.

INDEED

Love.

HARADRIM

Mummakan says that he is innocent, and that Herumor's accusation is false. He can only tell one lie, so both those have to be truth and he and Sangahyando are not guilty. Herumor and Dalamir both accuse Mummakan - a lie - and declare innocence, so they are not guilty. Therefore Fuinur is the guilty one.

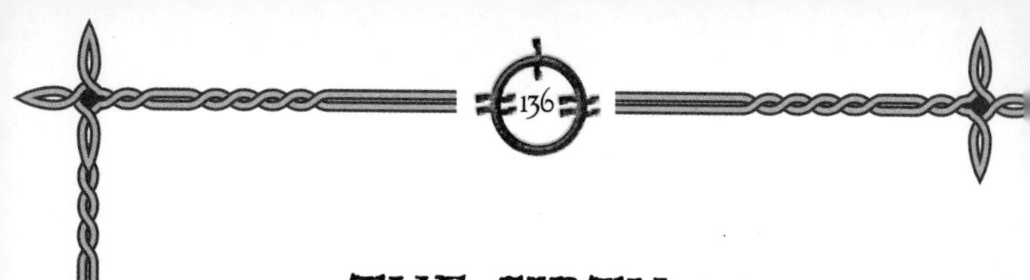

THE CIRTH 3

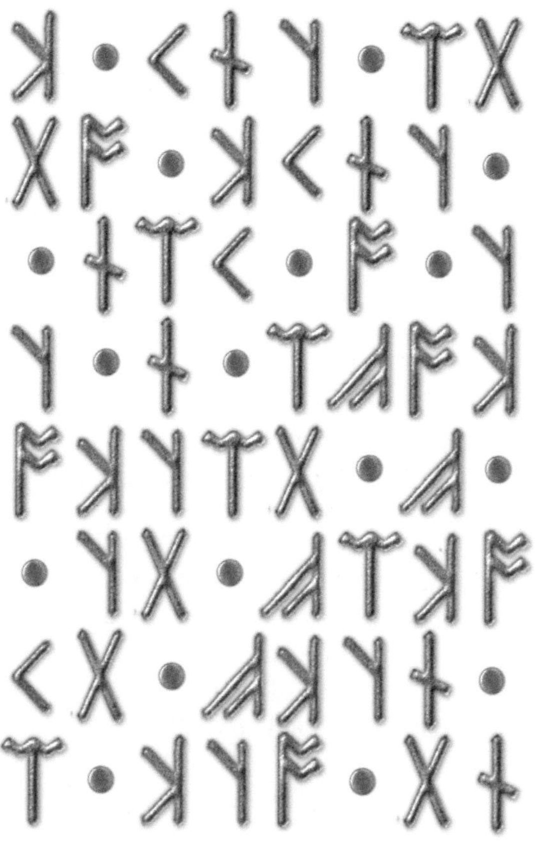

SIREN

Beer.

POST

The 4th. Going down and back up, the end posts are counted once, and the others twice, so one circuit is 12 posts. Divide 1000 by 12, and you get 83 full circuits, with 4 left over.

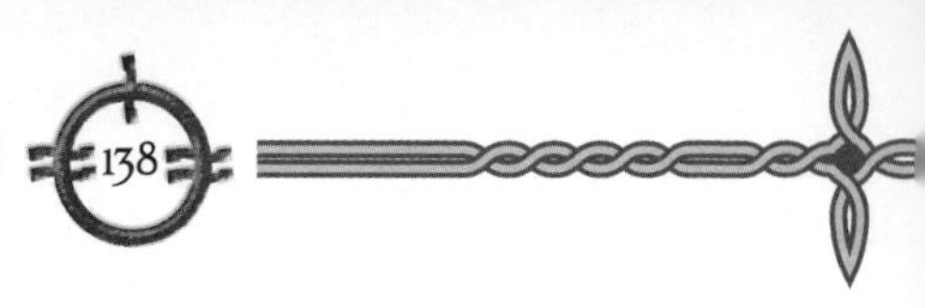

COOPERS

22 days. We know the average work-rates, and bearing in mind that each sum represents two men's work, then Egalmoth singly followed by Faren singly would take 32 days, and similarly E + P = 36 days, and F + P = 40 days. That gives us three simultaneous equations, and substituting through, we find that Egalmoth could do it in 14 days, Faren in 18 days, and Pelemir in 22 days.

SPITE

A flea.

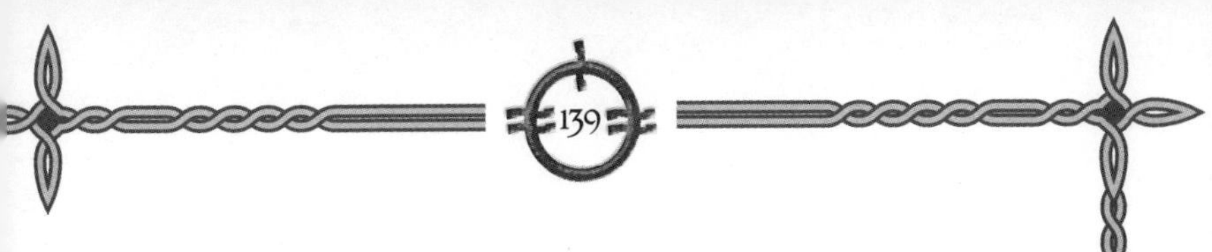

THE NINE

Two hours and 36 minutes. In the course of 1 hour, the carter can take 3 men 12 miles ahead, and come back 8 on his own. In the same time, the other 6 men will walk 4 miles, to meet him. Doing the same thing again, he takes 3 men from the 4-mile point to the 16-mile point, where the first group will be, returning to meet the last group at the 8-mile point. From there, it's just a straight 12-mile run to the end, taking 12/20ths of an hour, or 36m.

THE NINE REDUX

Five, of course - the dead ones.

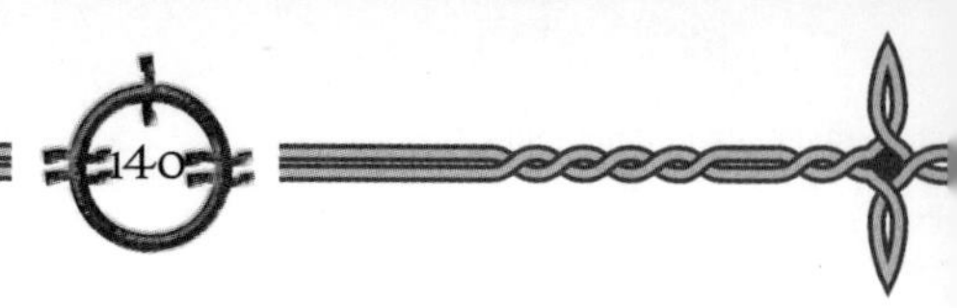

ANGMAR

200 men and 50 women. If x is female and y is male, then originally x + y = 250. If the increase factor in males is z, then (x + 3zx) + (y + zy) = 2,000. The increase factor z is 5, leading to an increase of 1,000 males and 750 females, meaning that the distribution now is 1200 male and 800 female.

CHOPPER

With the 50lbs weight on one side of the scale and the 90lbs on the other, you can measure a 40lbs heap. Do that four times, and the remaining wood will also weigh 40lbs. Then take off the weights, and split each stack between the two sides until they balance, giving you two 20lbs stacks.

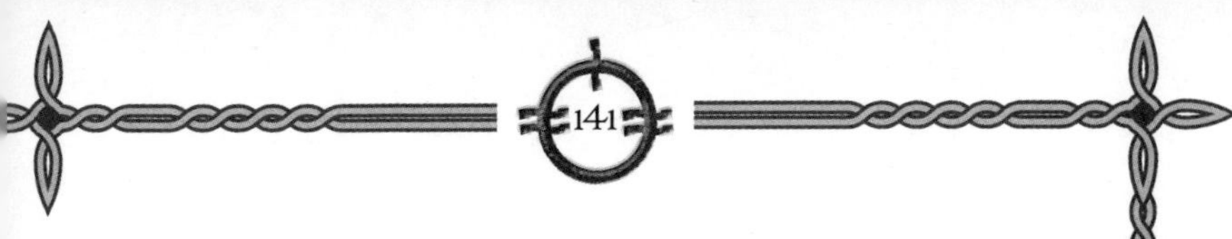

DUNGEONS

Yes, if you pass through the first door at 19m and 15s, no more than 9 seconds after opening your cell. The doors all run to a 35s beat, opening 3x, 2x, 5x, 4x and 1x that amount respectively. To get out, the doors have to open from first to last on successive beats, which takes 4x35s, or 2m 20s. The whole cycle, from open to open, takes 35 minutes, or 60 cycles. So to escape, the prisoner needs five sequential numbers from 0-60, divisible by 3, 2, 5, 4, and (trivially) 1. The only four numbers fitting the bill of the first four requirements are 33, 34, 35 and 36. So the escape point is at 33x35 = 1155 seconds. It'll probably be too late to cancel the alarm, however...

BUNCE

The answer can only be that Lily Bunce is 39, Andwise is 21, Nick and Largo are twins at 18, Angelica is 12 and Dora is 9.

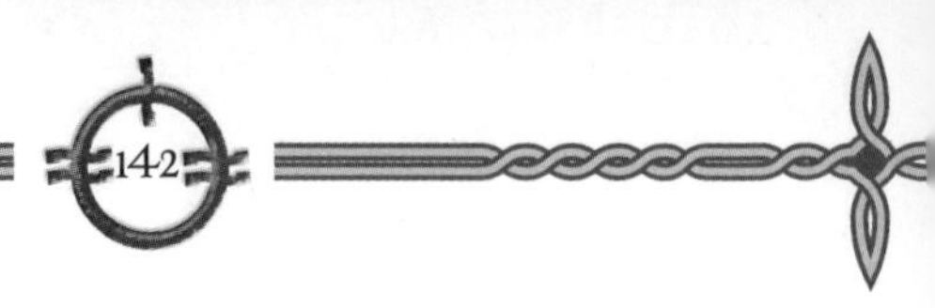

THE BALROG'S CURSE

The first five statements are true, the remainder false. The rule in problems of this sort is that so long as there are an even number of statements, half are true, the other half false - try thinking it through with just two statements. All other options become inconsistent. Odd numbers of statements have no valid logical solution.

CONFIDENCE

Tomorrow.

THE HOST

5,670 in the first, 6,615 in the second, 3,240 in the third, 2,730 in the fourth, and 2,772 in the fifth. Convert to equivalent fractions with a common numerator (the lowest common numerator is 630). This gives you first estimates of 1,890, 2,205, 1,080, 910 and 924. This is way too few; just 7,009. There are just over 21,000 orcs, so multiply your estimates by three.

CREATURE

A chisel.

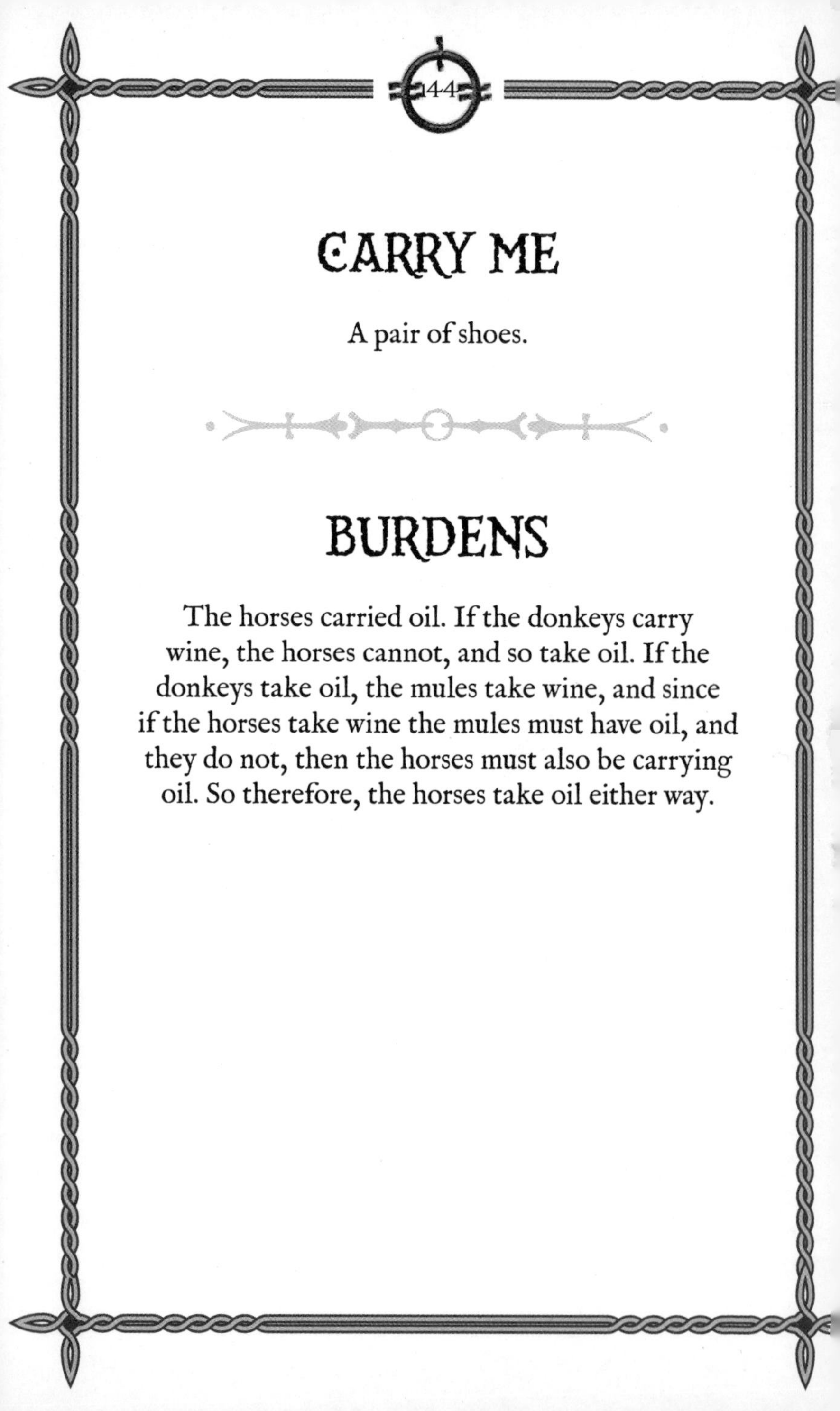

CARRY ME

A pair of shoes.

BURDENS

The horses carried oil. If the donkeys carry wine, the horses cannot, and so take oil. If the donkeys take oil, the mules take wine, and since if the horses take wine the mules must have oil, and they do not, then the horses must also be carrying oil. So therefore, the horses take oil either way.